Editor-in-Chief and Founder:
Lyndon H. LaRouche, Jr.
Editorial Board: *Lyndon H. LaRouche, Jr. , Helga
Zepp-LaRouche, Robert Ingraham, Tony
Papert, Gerald Rose, Dennis Small, Jeffrey
Steinberg, William Wertz*
Co-Editors: *Robert Ingraham, Tony Papert*
Managing Editor: *Nancy Spannaus*
Technology: *Marsha Freeman*
Books: *Katherine Notley*
Ebooks: *Richard Burden*
Graphics: *Alan Yue*
Photos: *Stuart Lewis*
Circulation Manager: *Stanley Ezrol*

INTELLIGENCE DIRECTORS
Counterintelligence: *Jeffrey Steinberg, Michele
Steinberg*
Economics: *John Hoefle, Marcia Merry Baker,
Paul Gallagher*
History: *Anton Chaitkin*
Ibero-America: *Dennis Small*
Russia and Eastern Europe: *Rachel Douglas*
United States: *Debra Freeman*

INTERNATIONAL BUREAUS
Bogotá: *Miriam Redondo*
Berlin: *Rainer Apel*
Copenhagen: *Tom Gillesberg*
Houston: *Harley Schlanger*
Lima: *Sara Madueño*
Melbourne: *Robert Barwick*
Mexico City: *Gerardo Castilleja Chávez*
New Delhi: *Ramtanu Maitra*
Paris: *Christine Bierre*
Stockholm: *Ulf Sandmark*
United Nations, N.Y.C.: *Leni Rubinstein*
Washington, D.C.: *William Jones*
Wiesbaden: *Göran Haglund*

ON THE WEB
e-mail: eirns@larouchepub.com
www.larouchepub.com
www.executiveintelligencereview.com
www.larouchepub.com/eiw
Webmaster: *John Sigerson*
Assistant Webmaster: *George Hollis*
Editor, Arabic-language edition: *Hussein Askary*

EIR (ISSN 0273-6314) *is published weekly
(50 issues), by EIR News Service, Inc.,
P.O. Box 17390, Washington, D.C. 20041-0390.
(703) 777-9451*

European Headquarters: E.I.R. GmbH, Postfach
Bahnstrasse 9a, D-65205, Wiesbaden, Germany
Tel: 49-611-73650
Homepage: http://www.eirna.com
e-mail: eirna@eirna.com
Director: Georg Neudecker

Montreal, Canada: 514-461-1557

Denmark: EIR - Danmark, Sankt Knuds Vej 11,
basement left, DK-1903 Frederiksberg, Denmark.
Tel.: +45 35 43 60 40, Fax: +45 35 43 87 57. e-mail:
eirdk@hotmail.com.

Mexico City: EIR, Sor Juana Inés de la Cruz 242-2
Col. Agricultura C.P. 11360
Delegación M. Hidalgo, México D.F.
Tel. (5525) 5318-2301
eirmexico@gmail.com

Canada Post Publication Sales Agreement
#40683579

Postmaster: Send all address changes to *EIR*, P.O.
Box 17390, Washington, D.C. 20041-0390.

Signed articles in *EIR* represent the views of the
authors, and not necessarily those of the Editorial
Board.

I0420567

Brunelleschi

EIR Contents

www.larouchepub.com Volume 42, Number 49, December 11, 2015

**Cover
This Week**

*Filippo
Bruneleschi and
perspective
drawing of the
Church of Santa
Maria del Santo
Spirito, Florence.*

Brunelleschi

Brunelleschi

Dec. 8—Lyndon LaRouche addressed associates in these terms on Tuesday, Dec 1.

There are two general subjects which are related ultimately, but which are distinctive; and I'm going to start with the first one on the subject of Filippo Brunelleschi (1377-1446). Now, what is not understood generally, is what Brunelleschi really was, and the depth of his work, and the importance of his work for all features of science; it was way beyond anything otherwise. Others in the same area of work were different; but he was very special in this respect, and on physical science, exceptional—absolutely exceptional. His breadth of understanding was great.

When you bring this into play, then you have to go back to Charlemagne, because you have to realize that there was a crisis which, after a great achievement by Charlemagne (742-814),—he had a short life, actually, and the span of his achievement was that—his own relatively short life. He had headquarters which travelled around the whole area of France and Germany; and this process was key to Brunelleschi, because he was responding to what Charlemagne had done before. And it was a different kind of discovery, but all of these discovery periods were divided by phases of degeneration.

For example, Nicholas of Cusa (1401-1464); what hap-

Architect Filippo Brunelleschi depicted looking up at his masterwork, the Duomo Santa Maria del Fiore, or cathedral dome of Florence. The sculpture was created by Luigi Pampaloni (1791-1847).

pened to him? Well, after him there was a degeneration of Christianity in that century and beyond. So, that kind of thing goes on again and again; and therefore, we cannot really try to derive from experience,—derive a principle on one principle as such, or a few principles. You can't do it; it doesn't work in history. History is a fairly long institution, relative to our own modest lives; and therefore we have to understand that we are actually operating between phases.

When Charlemagne was dead, the great achievements of Charlemagne disappeared. The water system,—Charlemagne created a water system; he did everything. It was a complete revolution, but when Charlemagne was dead, then the religious bodies in Europe destroyed the achievements that Charlemagne had accomplished; and it took several generations to get back to what Charlemagne had achieved. And it was never fully done itself; I mean, we had one system of water management in Germany in fact, and there was this connection in the water system—it was never finished. Even in modern times, it's still like that.

What No One Wants to Talk About

So therefore when you're talking about things, you cannot simply say, "This is our experience; this is what we've experienced," because you've got to think about the ups and downs of the history of mankind. The Charlemagne case is a typical one.

I mean, here's this guy, coming up on the edge of what we call Germany today, and France, who created a whole water management system which changed everything. And then it passed.

In the case of Brunelleschi, he was actually the most important figure in the development of physical experimental work in that period; he was. His work, which I have labored over, is great; it's unique. And Nicholas of Cusa is a different proposition, even though the consequences of connection are there.

So therefore, the problem is that we discuss being confronted with a new urgency on the basis of the Obama case. You can't take the Obama case *per se* and make that the story; because it has a precedent and it has a consequence. And the consequences are varied, and similarly other things. So, when we say, "We've got the latest facts; here are all the facts. This is what we said; we just discussed it all, it's all clear." Bunk! Absolute bunk! Because people don't recognize what is coming up as an effect, as a result of what had preceded. But people always want to say, "Let's be practical." And practical people are intrinsically idiots; at least when it comes to anything of importance. And this organization is no exception to this kind of problem.

For example, I'm an old man; I'm an ancient creature. I'm not Methuselah or anything like that, but I'm old. And my knowledge of history—which is not poor—warns me that you cannot proceed from recently adopted concepts of experience; you cannot use that as a standard for saying what the present is. If you don't know what the future was before, then you don't know anything about the present; you have an opinion about the present, but you don't have an efficient concept of the issue.

And Brunelleschi is typical of this kind of thing; he was actually the developer of physical science. It's what his effect was in every area; he was absolutely unique. And when he passed on,—when his movement passed on, his business passed on,—things began to crumble. And right now, if you wanted to come to a conclusion about what the situation is here in the United States, you probably would make the same great mistake of presuming that it started just yesterday. And that's where we are now.

And therefore we have to look at deeper things; we have to look at things that people don't like to talk about, because they like to talk about the things they like to talk about. And what they especially like to talk about is the crap. They say, "Oh! That's crap! Hey, come see the crap!" You try to reduce things to practical considerations; and practical considerations are the things that make idiots out of people. You cannot ignore history—living history; and most people do. They say, "Well, here are the facts. We can make a deductive conclusion based on this array of facts." But that's scientifically incompetent; and Brunelleschi is a good example of that principle, when you put in some other cases I've just mentioned as cases in history.

But what happens is, we accept certain common things that people treat as common opinion; and by sticking to those kinds of conceptions, they want to get up and say something. They want to say, "Well, this is a fact; this is a fact; this is a fact." Nonsense; it's not the fact. You have to go more deeply; like what we have to deal with, with China right now. We have to deal with everything in the Pacific area right now; we have to go to the history of China, as Leibniz explored it. If you haven't studied the work of Leibniz, you don't know anything about China. Who were the great leaders in China in that period? When Leibniz was alive? And Leibniz's influence in what he did there and elsewhere was the foundation of what was coming out of the past before.

So therefore, the problem we have, is we think we have a big mouth, and we can still get the words out and get people to agree with it. And what they're advising themselves is to hang themselves. Practical people are idiots. And you can say, "Well, what kind of baseball do you play?" Just another idiot? And that's what the problem is; we do not think enough. And if you look at the condition of our intellectual level, it is crap; most of it's crap. They don't have any attention to the root of reality—even current reality; and you can never understand current reality unless you look more deeply into the past. And that's the secret of finding out.

Don't 'Be Practical'

Just take Brunelleschi, for example; just make a list of his scientific interpretations and accomplishments. That list—very few people in the United States today have any idea of what that involved. So, that's where our problem lies.

And now we're coming in with the question of: "Is Obama going to be successful in destroying the human species?" That's your question; and that's the only question that's competent. How are we going to get rid of Obama so that we can have a continued human civilization? And you have to go at the root of things, not trying to make compromises by negotiation; that does not work. Only idiots do it; or idiots who are people who are totally unimportant, because we don't care what they say. Whatever they say is not important. But what happens, is we tend to make a social agreement with people. "Let's learn to adapt to each other." That doesn't work either; it's the best way of spreading syphilis.

So therefore we have to think seriously about this. Look, we're on the edge of the extermination of the human species; don't worry about who's talking about what, what kind of weapons and so forth. It doesn't make any damn difference. In less than twenty minutes, you're dead; and your death will have been announced and reported throughout the planet. How long does it take for a full-scale thermonuclear blast against a great nation? And what will remain as a result of that blast? Possibly, absolutely nothing, except waste.

And therefore, what do we have to do? Well, the simple thing is we say, "If we get rid of Obama, if we throw him out of office, this is a new story." And people say they're going to negotiate with Obama? That is real stupidity. If you're negotiating with Obama, you're a traitor to mankind. This man must be thrown out of office. And a sudden reform in the processes of the United States and other nations—particularly the transAtlantic area—has to go through a complete change; a sudden and complete change. There are no practical measures that can be taken; only decisive measures.

So, if you look at this thing from what I just listed as a few cases of history which are very familiar to me,—because I used to do a lot of that. But I know that if you don't understand the deeper part of the history of mankind, you don't know anything; you're just making wild guesses, whatever you say. And that's where we have to be careful. What's the root of the issue? And I can tell you that practically everyone in this nation is absolutely ignorant of those considerations; they have no conception whatsoever of how history is formed, of how history is generated. And people say, "Well, I had

Schiller Institute

The Schiller Institute's New York City Community chorus, rehearsing in September 2015.

an experience yesterday." "You had an experience yesterday? Well, why don't you clean it up?"

So, we've got to turn into that direction. And right, now what's the point? We have to have one thing; Obama must be dumped. You cannot negotiate with Obama; you have to dump him. There's no chance of winning, there's no chance of surviving if you want to play with that game, dump him. He's no good; he's a Satanic figure, just like his stepfather was. And probably his mother, too; she wasn't doing violent things in the same way, but she was uttering influences which amounted to the same effect.

The Manhattan Music Program

And therefore, we have to say, is: what's wrong with the mind of the present American personality, or the European personality; what's wrong with them? Why are they so stupid? And I can tell you they're very stupid; I'm an expert in knowing how stupid they are. Because they don't have any sense of the origin of the process from which results emerge; it's a lesson in history, it's a lesson in terms of science. It's a lesson in terms of everything. And that's why good history is so important; because unless you can look back into history—before Zeus, shall we say—but then the question is, how was Zeus controlled? He was controlled. Who did it; how was it done?

Well, you see the same thing is going on now; Wall Street is the same kind of thing. It's a destructive force which is making mincemeat out of people. And what are they doing? They're saying, "You've got to be practical." I said, "Well, when do you want to get the burial service?"

Therefore, we are not paying attention; we're looking at what we call the practical issues. And when you concentrate on the practical issues, you become an idiot; because you're so associated with these so-called practical issues, that you're completely blurred, and you have no idea of how history works—human history. It's like people say, "Well, you're talking about human beings." Well, human beings are not born as such. They evolve by a process of history; and sometimes the history is bad, and sometimes it's moderate. But that's what you have to understand; you have to understand Charlemagne. You have to understand these kinds of things; if you don't, you don't know anything. And that's where this fragmentation of experience destroys us.

And I can tell you, that most of what I get, most of the stuff is crap. Why? Because they're trying to be practical; they're trying to come to an agreement on what they think could work. And they assume that having said that, that all things are going to happen nicely, somehow or other.

What do we have? We have Manhattan; we also have some areas immediately around Manhattan. We are using what? We are using the Italian standpoint of musical composition. We are trying to gather together the kinds of instruments which are Classical instruments for that purpose, to build a group of people who are specialists, who will make this thing work. We are in a position to do it.

We've got to cut this crap out about being practical; and saying, "Well, people like this; people don't like that." I don't give a damn! What I care about is the past and future of human history; nothing else means anything, everything else is garbage. And you can know it for yourself when you think back about these things; about the failed life which people find themselves trapped into.

So, let's not get into the idea that we're going to say, "We've got the big solution for Obama's attempt to destroy this human race." That's not the way you go at it; you have to go at the historical root of the problem. If that's not your starting point, your actions are not competent.

What we're doing, is we're solving part of the problem by what we're doing in the musical program which we're developing in and around Manhattan. We have a few spots here and there of people who have some qual-

ity you can turn to as talent; but most of the people of the United States have no talent. The talent has been taken out of them since Bertrand Russell. So we've got to get more serious about it; the issue is clear.

I don't think our people really understand how deadly the present moment is. I mean, you have to take a measurement of what is the charge that is going to launch the war? How much? How many? What's Obama doing? What's the effect of his existence? You would say immediately, "Put him in prison. Put him in a prison cell, and shut him up. Let him talk to the walls; we don't want to hear what he has to say." And that's where the problem lies; we are not determined to get rid of him. It's easy; just simply do it. What he does, he blackmails people. How does he blackmail people? By death threats. How many people has he killed? How many Americans has he killed?

On the Tuesday events [Obama's Terror Tuesdays], how many Americans have gone down? And others gone down because of Obama? And you're sitting there and saying that Obama is the President; we have to respect him as a President? That's where the problem comes in. And point is, you have to look more deeply at the actuality of history. You've got to educate people so they actually understand history; not coming out with "I got it! I got this answer!" No. You've got to think more calmly and more profoundly; and think of history. If you don't know history, you don't know anything. So anyway, that's my concern....

History Doesn't Just Happen

How do you stop it, that's the point. How do you stop it? How do you stop the current course of history? Because everything, every problem of mankind is the failure to stop the bad history which is in the making. And that's where most people are screwed up. They say, what's a practical solution to this problem? And if you're not influencing the *future* thinking of the population, you ain't doing nothing. You're not doing anything important. The idea that,—you know,—history will tell you what the future is,—history does *not* tell you what the future is! Mankind's development determines what the future is.

And Brunelleschi is a good example of this. His work is an excellent model, because he was a leading figure in a crucial period of the Renaissance. His work was absolutely magnificent. And that's where you have to *generate* the future, not react against it. Generate the future.

And what we're up against is that. Now what we're doing is, how are we working? We're working basically on what? We're working on music; well, what're we doing about music? Well, we are not doing what most people think you should do in music. That you can't make a deductive process. A deductive notion of mankind's future is for idiots. You have to create the future, and you don't derive the future from the past. You free mankind *of* the past. You don't learn from the past, you learn to get out of it.

And that's exactly what is not happening since the beginning of the Twentieth Century, with Bertrand Russell's operation in particular, what's the direction in which mankind is going? Down! *Down!*

These are the problems, and the fact is that we're not intelligent enough, and we haven't learned from history. I spent most of my activity in learning history, ancient history, all kinds of history. And you're looking for the change, which *is* history. And it's not something that happened to you; it's something that you pushed, and made happen.

And if you don't have that sense of pushing to make something happen, which must be made to be caused to happen, then you're a failure, and your opinions are a failure. You don't try to deduce facts. You smear the facts, you say, "facts, facts!" You want to talk to me about "facts"!? You want to die in your cemetery? You want to die in your tomb, is that what you want? Is that your future? You're waiting till you can complete your death? When your nuisance value will be over.

The question is, how do you create the necessary future? And that is the nature of mankind's achievements. But you go into the schoolroom: "Well, history has taught us. . ." What do you mean history has "taught us"? Did you teach that? Did you teach the future? Well, who teaches the future? Very few people, very rare people. And when a crisis occurred in the course of history, what happened? Then history as a process as a whole, collapsed!

And that's my nightmare concern.

I've been going a good deal around the world in the course of my life, and that's what I've learned: You don't learn from experience. You are forewarned of the stupidity of your inclination to think that you know what the future is, in terms of what's already happening. When you say, "a trend direction" is the future,

Brunelleschi depicted holding a model of the dome of the Florence cathedral, by Italian painter Giuseppe Bezzouli (1784-1855).

then you're in trouble. And that's what happens to people. You have to be the adventurer, to go where others have never gone before. And that's what this organization has to be able to do, otherwise we cannot win this one.

I *hate* practical people, not as a personal business, but I hate the fact that they exist. The disaster that's going to come as a result of that.

And this Brunelleschi is probably, for the present time,—Brunelleschi's achievements in science in many different ways, are a good model to understand how the future is created. That's what he was: He created the future. He created the very idea of music; people didn't know what music was until he came along. And he has this nice little place there [the Pazzi Chapel], where you go into this place, and here it is, the thing is alive! Here's this small instrument there, and it's alive, it's music. It's a piece of genius. And that's what you're looking for.

It's Made to Happen

Anyway, so that's the picture. And I say let's be conscious about this thing. Let's not be practical. Let's not say, "so and so said such and such." Forget it! Most people who I know of who are authorities are incompetents. So what do you want to listen to them for?

If you do not have the insight to see the future,

you're not competent. And that should be the purpose of education. But the practical people will kill you. Don't listen to practical people. Anyway, that's our issue, that's what the issue is,—that we really have to have an understanding of how we shape the future. How do we change the mood of the people in the United States, from the stupidity which is their characteristic trait right now?

They're out there; they've taken their position, and they're deciding to rely upon orders by Obama. They're saying: "Obama is making the policy, this is Obama's policy." What do you want to do with people who have that idea? Put 'em into prison. And tell 'em never to talk, they might spread a disease.

So you see the future, as the future, and the future is what's wrong with the present. So when someone says he's an expert, "Uh-oh, one of those guys, huh? We never were able to clean up their confusion."

And this is the nightmare that I have, always this stuff: Somebody comes along, "Well experience shows

The Pazzi Chapel

Dec. 8—Italian soprano Antonella Banaudi told a Feb 26, 2012 Schiller Institute conference in Berlin: "I recently went to the Pazzi Chapel, in Florence of course, the Florence of Brunelleschi and Ficino. In its naked proportion and simplicity, in the balance of light and colors, it gave a beautiful resonance to the sound of my voice: a demonstration that it is the proportion, the idea translated into construction, that resonates inside of us. The emotion I felt in hearing a response from the stone, that almost supported me in singing,—as if the stone were alive, and expressing itself through cosmic vibration,—made me feel part of a whole that unites stone and man, in a harmony that is the reason for the existence of everything. It is the same harmony that we seek and experience when singing together, playing together, participating in a sort of rite/celebration that is beyond religion, and is profoundly moral and human."

Brunelleschi's Pazzi Chapel, located in the Church of Santa Croce in Florence, Italy.

In the same connection, Lyndon LaRouche remarked to the Dec. 1 meeting reported elsewhere in this issue, that "It was in all dimensions of this. Like this little chapel; you walk into that chapel [the Pazzi Chapel], Helga and I walked into this chapel, and the whole thing was like a living creature. You're just in there. You were seized by this little chapel; it gripped you. You couldn't get free of it! You have to get out of it in order to see something else that was there, but it was like the whole thing was a living process. And that was his quality of work; everything he did was absolutely unique, and highly variegated and so forth.

"And that's what we have to look in ourselves for, in order to understand what we must do in dealing with the crisis which comes on us immediately right now."

us…", "He has an opinion…", "You should listen to his opinion…",—my God, it drives me wild.

So our job is to do this. I think we're potentially doing well, but I think we get sucked into trying to propitiate idiots. We try to say, "well, they will agree to this, they will agree with that…" Nah! Forget it, it's all crap!

And what we're doing with the music thing is what is the key. Now, we cannot do much with music on a continental basis. The musical capabilities of the population of the United States are very, very, very, very, very poor. If they ever had a musical insight, they lost it somewhere along the line, dropped in a garbage pail or something like that.

But what we're doing, is we go back to the Italian,—for example we're using the Italian model now. It has several attributes which are extremely important, including that we have a bunch of musicians who are more or less still running around in the Manhattan area, Brooklyn, and so forth. And if we pull those instrumentalists into the kind of thing that these instruments were *designed* to do, according to the Italian standpoint,—Ah! Now you've got something!

Because what you're doing is, you are attacking the failure. Therefore you say, how do we tune this? So the point is, the key thing is, how do you tune the mind of the human individual? How do you tune the process of their development, of their ability to make these creative, recreative processes? So that's what we have.

So you have this one area,—there's something in Manhattan,—pieces in Manhattan, only pieces. We're going into this larger part of the area, where we have these instruments which are being re-tuned, to fit the Italian standard.

And this is a language which is otherwise not spoken. So you want to get rid of the other kind of music, and that's what the tuning process means. And what we do,—we can do it. I would say now,—I would say,—well, in two years we could do it, because there are a lot of instruments that have to be fixed; people have to do the things properly; we have to check the whole process. That has to be gone through.

But we already have access to this. We have some work on music, vocal music in particular, and instrumental as well. We have that access open to us, so we will make the best we can out of it. And we will try to discover what we lost, or what we lost which was the future. That's the way we have to approach this thing.

The Principle of Brunelleschi

Dec. 8—A participant in Lyndon LaRouche's nationwide Fireside Chat conference call of Thursday, Dec 2, asked him, "What is the relationship between the mind of an individual human being and the collective human mind? The individual mind is associated with an individual body. When the body dies, so does some part of the individual mind that may be called the personality. The collective human mind does not die, but rather progresses to higher and higher levels of comprehension. Each individual that is born may be said to begin at the level of comprehension that the human mind has reached up to that time. But how does the human mind progress,—that is advance beyond the past, beyond what is known into the unknown?"

LaRouche answered, "Okay, I've got an answer for this boy which I think is quite appropriate in particular. It's something I just did in reporting and putting into print on Tuesday. And what I did, is I went through the history of a famous man of his time, Brunelleschi. And Brunelleschi was one of the great geniuses in the whole history of mankind, who created the understanding of how mankind creates the future.

"And what had happened, is that idea, the principle of Brunelleschi, who is the greatest educator in terms of scientific method on record so far,—other people were great physicists and so forth, but he was very special. He really created the launching of the physical-economic features of the Renaissance. Without that, it would not have occurred. And you have to understand that, because the issue is that you don't inherit from one generation or one period of culture to another. That is not the way that mankind actually progresses, and the history has shown that repeatedly.

"What there is, is that there are fresh discussions, or a fresh view of what mankind is capable of doing, and Brunelleschi did that. He was absolutely a genius in this matter. I think there was no one like him in that time, in quality of action. And so I think perhaps a careful attention to the case of Brunelleschi would be a very powerful influence.

Perspective drawing for the Church of Santa Maria del Santo Spirito by Filippo Brunelleschi.

generation which is the characteristic of the Twentieth Century and beyond. And Bertrand Russell, of course, is the typical agent who typifies that degeneracy. We are living in the United States under a degenerate culture. Now we have to end that degenerate culture, by replacing it with a higher, a proper generation of culture,—as Brunelleschi did in his lifetime. Brunelleschi did things that nobody else was able to do, among all the people around him. He's a *remarkable* genius,—and it's the remarkable factor of genius among great minds,— and his accomplishments were *immense*. And that's the way you have to look at it.

"See, mankind does not go by inheritances as such; it does not work that way. Think: inheritances come and go. Whole regimes come and go. And it seems to be the case that they're interrupted, totally,—that they're not continuous. And that's true!

"So therefore, there is a time where mankind acts to *create* these kinds of forces, and it seems to come from a mystery. But the idea that you 'learn from experience,' that you are informed by being stimulated by experience, is not true. I mean, the collapse of whole systems of government in the history of mankind as we've known it, is full of complete breakdowns. But mankind has recovered. And it is people who became creative forces in their own right who made this kind of thing possible.

"And that's what we have to look at. That's the idea you have to see. Forget the idea about being 'practical!' The idea of being practical in terms of generations, and generations,—we have to be practical,—nonsense! I can tell you one thing, that the generation of the people of the United States, since the beginning of the Twentieth Century to the present time, has been one of degeneration!

"Now, what we've got to do, is we've got to reverse that problem. We've got to eliminate the factor of de-

"We have to take our children, we have to take those we're educating, and we have to get them to see what they can do, the miracles that they can develop and create as a result of their passion for the progress of mankind.

"There is no such thing as an evolutionary process of development of human culture. There are *effects* which occur at certain times. But then, suddenly, the whole culture collapses, vanishes, it's slaughtered. Then later, somebody else arrives, stimulates something new, and gives mankind another chance at progress.

"And our job is to understand this question of progress, and progress is not an evolutionary process. It's always a *revolutionary* process, it is never evolutionary! And everybody who's sitting around waiting for a revolutionary process is just kidding themselves. A revolution of that type has to be an act of genius, which comes as if from nowhere. But that's the way mankind succeeds. And I'm looking for people who will do that kind of work, and become the geniuses who cause the future to be reborn again.

The Brunelleschi Principle

Dec. 8—*This is excerpted from the internet broadcast of Lyndon LaRouche's discussion with the LaRouche PAC Policy Committee on Dec 7.*

Diane Sare: Good afternoon. It's Monday, Dec. 7, 2015, known by some as Pearl Harbor Day; I'm Diane Sare and I'm filling in for Matthew Ogden, and we are joined over YouTube by Bill Roberts, from Detroit, Michigan; Dave Christie and Mike Steger who are both in San Francisco, California; Kesha Rogers, from Houston, Texas; and Rachel Brinkley from Boston, Massachusetts. And here in the studio, we have Ben Deniston and Jason Ross from the LaRouche PAC Science Team, and of course, Mr. LaRouche.

And I imagine you have some words for us:

Lyndon LaRouche: Yes, I do. On the beginning of the past week, on Tuesday, I 'in-completed' a thing that I was doing, because it got out of order. But what I did was present the actual case of Brunelleschi; and Brunelleschi's importance in the whole history of science is unique. So he's not something like a fill-in in any sense; he created a completely new conception of what mankind's mental powers are. And nothing had ever been done like that, up to that time, that we know of,— maybe scattered things, or so forth,—in history.

But what the problem today is, that most people have no understanding,—even people who are called scientists have no comprehension whatsoever of what Brunelleschi's work was based on. And I spent a good deal of my life, both in direct education on this thing, and also in doing research, which I did with my friends in Italy who were specialists in this also. And so, even to this day, the average person has no comprehension of the princi-ples of science of Brunelleschi. It's just backwards. What happened is, of course, the collapse after Nicholas of Cusa; he was pushed aside from history for that time, and the whole thing was a terrible thing.

And Leibniz played a very crucial role in repairing that damage, but it was not adequate. He did a great job, but it was not adequate on this point. And so therefore, I had spent a lot of my life, from that point on, on

creative commons/sailko

Brunelleschi's dome, as seen from the bell tower nearby.

Brunelleschi. And most people today,—even though Brunelleschi is a well-known name among scientists,—the interpretation of his work is often mixed up, screwed up.

A New Factor in History

Because the difference is that people think that history can be recorded as a simple continuity. That does not work. Because most of history is breaks, breaks in human history; and evil periods and broken periods came into existence in the history. And so then what Brunelleschi did, was that he brought in a concept of science, which is unique in terms of what is known today. Most people who were educated in this,

Brunelleschi's dome in its Florentine setting.

have no comprehension whatsoever of what Brunelleschi did. It's all available there for people, if they were to study it enough; and it was brilliant. It was absolutely unique. And so I would say today, the problem is that in our organization in itself, and other locations, that the lack of understanding of the work of Brunelleschi is the reason for the source of the stupidity shown by even many of our own members in this thing. And therefore, it's extremely important that we realize that we are facing a great change threatening us. And the Obama Administration is an example of the great danger to the existence of the human species.

And this kind of thing which is expressed by the work of Brunelleschi, is actually the solution, the key to the solution to understand actually how things were intended to work.

And so we have mostly in our organization, our organization has no real comprehension; most members have no comprehension of what Brunelleschi did, of the importance of what he did. Even though all the work is published, it's there and so forth, but it's not done. And therefore, I think, one of the things that is a weakness in our own organization, is our failure to understand an actual comprehension of Brunelleschi.

Sare: Well there are two aspects of his work that I was reflecting upon this week, as you were speaking and discussing it. One is his design which is perhaps the most famous of his work, which is the Dome in Florence, where people have assumptions, like your

wife referenced the Communist Party wanting to fill in the holes; but his understanding of harmonic ordering principles of the Universe, and also the necessity of having more than one principle, as Kepler did as well, which is not just visual, but it's two senses, you could say. And the assumption by people who haven't done this work, or haven't studied it, is that it was just,—things didn't precisely mesh, and therefore he made a mistake, or he didn't know what he was doing. As opposed to saying perhaps the people making that assertion are the ones who don't know what they're doing, because they haven't bothered to try and understand the principles of the Universe, as a living, developing growth process.

LaRouche: The problem is also, more particularly, the lack of a continuity in the experience, even under his work. He was not wrong in anything he did, but the people who have studied him often are completely mistaken. Because what happens, is, as I emphasized in my remarks on this last Tuesday,—is that you introduce a new factor in history. And what I laid out on Tuesday,—what I started to lay out there,—is that all these things do not have a continuity.

Why? Because if you look at the actual history of nations, you'll find there are breaks, very significant breaks; of Charlemagne is an example, all these kinds of things, they were all breaks, so there was no continuity! So the idea that you know the past, on the basis of your experience of a trend in things,—but the trend is not the maker. And Brunelleschi made it very clear, that you had to get rid of all these assumptions that there's a continuity in history, a simple continuity, where one part of the society goes to the next part of society. What there is, in fact, has been great breaks, like Brunelleschi, who has concentrated on that issue, the great breaks in history up to that time.

And most people have no understanding, and I think most members of our own organization have no comprehension of what this issue is. They don't understand him. What happened later, at that point, when he was dead, he'd been freshly dead,—people just lost it, they had no comprehension. You got implications of that from Kepler. You have implications from Kepler in particular; but especially, Leibniz. Leibniz is the great figure, who actually gives you the greatest degree,—and Shakespeare,—gives you the greatest degree of continuity of mankind, for the span of Shakespeare's life. He had a comprehension of this kind of thing.

Sare: Well, the other point that came to mind was that people think of this Dome as being part of the architecture of the church. But, if you go to Florence, what you discover is that the Dome is the architecture of the entire city; that it has actually created a certain dynamic, because of its presence. So it wasn't just an organization of the church, per se; it was actually an organization of the population of the time. And to the present, because it has that effect even to this day.

All Progress is in Leaps

LaRouche: He was the only one who had the competence to do that. [laughter] That's the fact of the matter! He had this particular competence. And nobody among his contemporaries had any systemic comprehension of this. None.

But the point is that what he represents with his method, is the only valid method for trying to understand what mankind today, means. That's where the problem comes in. And they all say they want to be practical. They want to pass examinations. They want to get this....

So what I'm stressing,—I will go back at this, and get this thing pushed through, at least in a simplified way so that the members understand something about these things. Because most of our members have no comprehension of what the meaning of all this is!

They don't have enough history, for example. If you don't know people in history, leaders in history, you really don't understand what the whole story's about. Because the breaks are very important. And even come up to modern times, for example, the importance of these developments is unknown. Even people in Germany who were involved in developing the water system, had up till that time, no understanding of what this was all about.

And so what the greatest problem is, is that we have people who say they're scientists, or at least they're experts simply, and they don't know what they're talking about. Because they don't understand that there are breaks in man's knowledge in the course of history. And it's extremely important today, that we have an understanding of that now, because we're dealing with a global process. And you cannot understand the global process, unless you understand how the breaks in history function to shape the way that history actually works.

Jason Ross: The need for Brunelleschi, at least for what he had done at the Dome, had been set up actually a half-century earlier, when the decision had been made to build the Cathedral, in such a way that eventually, that sort of Dome would be required, even though no one at the time knew really how to build it.

So then, when Brunelleschi entered the competition, and when he was chosen to complete and build the Dome....

LaRouche: He had a great sense of humor about that.

Ross: He really did! Because people said, why should we give you the contract? How are you even going to build this? And instead of telling them, he told them a joke about why they weren't able to think properly to be able to figure it out, but that he knew what to do. And then when he did go through with it, the approach that he took was one that was very important for what Kepler did later. Brunelleschi's approach to it was not to approach architecture from the standpoint of geometry, but from physics: That you can try to make a shape that you would like to have, but maybe the bricks and the stones won't agree with that. You actually have to.... [laughter]

LaRouche: That's where the Kepler leap comes into play. You come at a certain point in the century, a difference. And what had proceeded from his work, now you find in Kepler,—you find again the consequence. Then you get a leap again with Leibniz, and so forth. So, therefore, if we don't understand the leaps in history, ... you know, the organization of society collapses; repeatedly, it collapsed! But somebody brings it back, but it doesn't bring it back as a continuity. It becomes a new development, which becomes the liberation, which frees you from the weakness of the preceding culture.

And that's what you do, like dealing with a Galactic problem today: The Galactic thing, as against Kepler, is a leap.

And you have other things that are leaps. And you can see this in the system. And if we're going to be efficient, as human beings, to deal with the challenges that mankind faces in space, you have to change your view from looking at it as: "I'm a man; my people remember certain things. These is the way *this* society, led step-by-step-by-step, to that point of launching."

Achievements of the Dead

And that does not work! You have to shift your identity from being that you are creating something just because you're a man at that time, and you have to realize that what you're actually doing,—you have to shift your point of view to the *higher* portion, the *whole*, as opposed to the detail. And that's where the problem is.

And that's what happens today: people, they are practical people, and they are therefore stupid people. Because they may have knowledge, but they don't have knowledge of the process by which mankind progresses. If you can't understand the Galaxy today, you really don't understand science.

And now we have to take the challenge of: what's the Galaxy mean? Or what's the galactic series, which is another, more complicated version of the whole thing; but that's the principle; that's not the complication, that's the principle.

Ben Deniston: It goes to what mankind really is as a creative species. You know, I think what you're saying, is that the practical way is treating mankind as if you're an animal or something, an animal species. You'd be saying, well, to solve the current crisis, we need to just look back at what we did before, and then re-establish what we had prior. Versus, the very idea of mankind is that we can always create ourselves anew, at a higher level.

But I think your emphasis on the idea of the breaks, I think is critical, because it is,—it's a non-continuity; the creation of a fundamentally higher state of existence, which doesn't really have a continuity from the other one, and that's, I think, a reflection of what *real* creativity is; what a real creative process is, of the generation of something new, which is the product of what the human mind can do, uniquely.

LaRouche: Exactly...

Deniston: The human mind has this unique ability to create a new physical existence in the universe, which would never exist without the action of the human mind, specifically to do that. And that's the substance of what enables mankind to move forward.

LaRouche: And that defines the meaning of mankind. Without that, you don't get it, so you get leaps. So you get leaps. So if you take Vernadsky, you have one thing, but you have an apparent leap, but it's not really a leap as such, it's a culmination of something that breaks loose, as if it had a different significance.

And so you can trace the thing with Brunelleschi, you can trace—well, his antecedents, by going back to his antecedents, you can get a better understanding of what he accomplished.

But the point is, the accomplishment.... With the personality of human beings, you can't say that you located it in the person as such; the living person who dies,—that is not the way you can define the problem. You have to find the connection which creates the leap into progress, as opposed to a continuity. You don't know what the process is, until you live it and find out what the mystery is; it's sort of: when you go to Kepler, you get a leap; when you go to the Galactic System, you get a leap. You get all kinds of leaps in the Solar System and through the whole thing itself. And it's the understanding that this is *the mind of man* which is creating mankind, not the other way around.

And the problem is: people running around and just saying, "well, I died," or something. And that is not the meaning of life. And people saying, "well, he had a good life, and that meant this...." is not a good consequence. Because it's that things burst free as if in pulsation, and you find people die; then you find people who have died, and they made the leaps in terms of what they accomplished by the effect of their own life. And there was no real evidence there that shows you a continuity; until you look backwards.

And when you look backwards, *now* you see what the connection was. But you didn't know if beforehand. You only knew it as some signal in terms of the social process, and then you recognize that something new had been introduced. Like Leibniz, for example, did that. And also some other great people did that in the same way.

So mankind is able to reflect on what mankind has accomplished when an interim period occurs. Then you are able to discover something, by recognizing it, when before you had been unable to recognize it. And the idea of the recognition of the future is what's important; that's where the continuity lies.

No One Else Ever Did This

Sare: You definitely don't want to continue in a linear fashion. Because if you say that where we're going has to be based on this current trend-line, then we know where we're going, which is the extinction of the human race: So it really is urgently necessary for people to have a conception of a break and a conception of a change in direction, which is a break from what you think is your current status.

LaRouche: Einstein. Einstein made several breaks in his development of his work. Breaks! Actual breaks. And the world around him was completely ignorant of the significance of those breaks. And he understood. With each case, he made a discovery, and the discoveries were successive; but the impulse for doing those kinds of things was there within him. And when he died, we lost track of what he had accomplished.

And that's where the problem arises. And the problem we have as an organization: we have a bunch of people who think they're "smarties." They think that they know things; they think they know things when they don't understand *this* issue! What is the progress of mankind? What do we mean by the "progress of mankind"? And that's where the failure is.

People say, "well, you have to be practical." And when someone says, "you have to be practical," I say, "you're stupid." And I'm right, every time, right on the mark! [laughter] And it's not modesty, it's honesty. So it's not a question of modesty, it's a question of honesty: You shouldn't argue things that ain't true. [laughter]

So I think this is what I'm concerned about right now, because we can do that, and of course I did a lot of

The tomb of the Holy Roman Emperor Charlemagne, built between 1182 and 1215 in the Aachen Cathedral, which Charlemagne had commissioned during his reign (800-814).

it when I was working in Italy, in particular. We were working on a lot of things of this nature, and we were having a grand old time! We were going out near this area where the Cathedral is, and I just had fun all the time with this thing! It's just—you know, it's something you *enjoy doing*. It's something you are gratified by the fact you were able to *do* something, to make a discovery.

Deniston: It seems as if you can look at the Twentieth Century in two phases: You know, people I think maybe more immediately, might recognize the more recent past two generations, where there's been no growth—we haven't developed fusion power, we haven't developed nuclear power. People look back and say, it took 50 years to go from the first flight, first airplane to going to the Moon. And it's been 50 years since we've gone to the Moon, and now we're nowhere. And it's a reflection of just this "no progress."

But I think what you're raising, is that this is kind of the effect, the result, of two generations prior, when you had this attack on something more fundamental; those are the expressions. The deeper issue is, what is society's self-recognition of the creative powers of the human mind in mankind? And that's what you saw viciously attacked with Russell; that's what Einstein was holding out against.

You've obviously spent much of your career, you've

often referenced that you got a lot of your start going against this "information theory," and cybernetics, all of this being an attack on recognizing creativity as a true principle, as a true substance; this type of creativity which creates these breaks, we're talking about, and how that was just viciously attacked in this earlier period around the turn of the century, into the postwar period.

And then this later effect we're having, of people accepting the green movement; you know, people accepting that! People accepting shutting down our space program, not going with nuclear power. That's an effect of this earlier process, which erased the recognition of what makes mankind different from other forms of life on this planet. An actual insight and recognition of that. That's what we have to return to, waging the fight on that battle, not just the effects of that process.

LaRouche: One of the processes in this whole thing which is crucial, is that people become defensive, because they're up against popular opinion, a formation of popular opinion by societies. And they have these things they believe in, these ideas they believe in as we see in various parts of society. And you realize that they have no conception of what we would call, legitimately, the progress of mankind. Not mankind as something there, but the process of development of mankind's accomplishments.

And it comes out in the form of leaps. Brunelleschi was really unique in this respect; nobody else ever accomplished anything like what he did, no one had ever accomplished it that way. And you had things from Leibniz, you actually got things from other sources of the same kind of thing. But the idea of the location of man's creative powers, that's where the problem comes up: they don't recognize what mankind's powers are, as a continuity. The continuity is not an event; the continuity is the process which generates events, progress.

And therefore, when we put people in schools, we educate them in schools, and they become idiots. Why? Because the dog didn't teach them any better! [laughter]

Man is Not of the Flesh

Rachel Brinkley: You see the correct principle of education in the Pazzi Chapel, which you've also brought up, that Brunelleschi created, which was—you made the point that you "sing" to it, and it "sings" back to you. And you also said Brunelleschi got rid of straight lines, which is funny, because an architect uses a lot of straight lines. But he created a geometry that was—an architectural structure that was a harmonic principle, or you sing to it, and it sings back to you.

And then Kepler later brought up this idea, built on the idea of harmony, saying also that harmony is not something that's in the terms, but it's in the mind. The comparison of the terms in the mind, so it's a process in action. So there are also no straight lines there. So you get the idea that he employed a principle which was unobservable, and he made it visible that you could only see when you sing, in his structure.

LaRouche: Yeah. That's exactly true. That's exactly how it works.

And you see what's wrong with education in the Twentieth Century, and beyond. And therefore, if you can't attack the Twentieth Century, as a practice, for its practice, then you become incompetent, and that's where the problem comes up. You try to say, "well, I worship an evil god," that's what it amounts to saying! Wall Street worships only evil gods! [laughter] And how do we get rid of those evil gods?

It's like Satan, you know, for example. I think many people in Manhattan find Satanists are running loose in the community.

Michael Steger: That's for sure. You also raised this question of Leibniz in China, in this discussion of Brunelleschi. And there's something unique, because if mankind survives into the Twenty-First Century, it will be because of the process of development that China has now initiated, which really does come from Leibniz's own insights into China; but then the follow-through and development of that by you and your wife Helga, in introducing those concepts into China's orientation, which have created the potential for a break. And if any nation is dedicated to a Brunelleschi-like development, at this point on the planet, it's China.

And really, the lack of courage, the lack of commitment of the American people to take on Obama, to take on this Satanic quality, if that can be provoked or inspired, which is I think somewhat what you're getting at with this "leap" question, this commitment to what mankind is, then you have the potential to consolidate that orientation, a Brunelleschi-like orientation on the planet today. But the lack of that courage, that cowardice of the American people, is the destruction of genius. It's the destruction of creativity: And that *has* to be addressed. That's the strategic failure today, in the United States, this recognition of what mankind truly is.

LaRouche: Exactly! Mankind is not of the flesh. Mankind's flesh is merely a conveyance, to move things from one place to the other. It is the effect, not the cause. And when mankind sees that mankind *is* the causal factor, not the other way around. And therefore, you don't want people to become stupid. And the practice of society in schools today, as in California, in the educational system, is to make people stupid. I think Hollywood is probably an example of that. In order to become successful you had to be stupid, that is, Hollywood-style.

On the Edge of a Vacuum

Kesha Rogers: I wanted to say, on this principle of the building of beautiful cities,—that's been a subject-matter that's come up quite a bit. The one thing that caught my attention when you brought up the whole discussion about Brunelleschi, is the idea and the principle, embodied in what is necessary to bring mankind and bring a culture,—from, as we've seen with the United States' current culture of complete degeneracy,—up to the standards which would be even understood and necessary for how you actually create cities which exemplify the true meaning of human existence, and human creativity? And we don't have that standard right now.

So even if we talk about the development of these great projects and building beautiful cities, it only would start from linear building blocks of a process,—versus actually, when you brought up Brunelleschi, one of the things that came to my attention was, "Wow, well, why wouldn't we have everything start from having created a cathedral built from this very Brunelleschian principle that would expand out, and

creative commons/Andrew Gray
Statue of Gottfried Leibniz (1646-1716) at the Oxford University Museum of Natural History.

every part of your city would be built from that foundation; which would start with a totally revolutionary principle in terms of the development of mankind overall?"

So that was something I was thinking about: is that what you just brought out, is something that bears on how we take people out of this degenerate state, and actually revolutionize our thinking about the upshifts in the progress of mankind in that very realm.

LaRouche: Yes. It's quite relevant.

Steger: Well, it seems to be also the same idea in principle governing what you've done with the Manhattan project, Lyn, the same kind of concept of what we're generating, and developing that as a unified characteristic of a nation, from a higher principle.

LaRouche: Exactly: That's what I think is essential for me, to do! Is exactly that. Because most people in society today, in the trans-Atlantic region and others, don't have any comprehension, of what the meaning of the human mind is. They just don't have it. They see it's a shadow, all they see is a shadow, they don't see a substance.

Now the substance is not of the flesh, it's not of material as such, *as such*. But the effect reveals itself as an effect. And once you say, "this was an effect," not "this was the truth, or this was the actuality," it's the *effect*, as such; and that's what you get with Brunelleschi. All his work was all of that nature. He was a man way ahead of all of his time, way ahead! And his creativity was forceful, and Kepler depended actually on the implication of the radiation of Brunelleschi. He would never have accomplished it without Brunelleschi.

And when Kepler got onto this question about the Solar System as such, he got into a completely new area. Then he died; Leibniz was born shortly after that, relatively speaking, and then you have the development of Leibniz. Then you have the death of Leibniz. And you had an anxiety, because there was no new Leibniz That's what happened; we had approximations of people who had these kinds of skills. But Leibniz was irreplaceable.

And everybody was awed, all the evil people were awed—"is he going to die! Is he going to die? Is he going to *die*?" And they were all betting on his dying.

But what they did, is they took the idea of his death, and said, "This is removed." What he had accomplished: "This is removed, history has ended. History is shut down." And you had, in history,—you got lots of these things of collapsed culture, and the people of those cultures, were dead, in general—dead! Then somebody would come along in a new Renaissance, and in that condition somebody would rediscover what had been lost. And so the history of mankind is a series of leaps of this nature, where society seems to make progress, and then fails. There's a gap; there's no newness to the whole process. Then, time passes, and if you're lucky, then you get a new Renaissance. And if the Renaissance is not sustained, then you get another vacuum.

And what we're living in, is we're living on the edge of a vacuum, which can be a source of destruction of mankind, unless we change our ways and fill in what Brunelleschi did in his way. Because when Brunelleschi had died, and Cusa had also died, you had a period of the most evil religious beliefs, lasting a whole century. Until Leibniz emerged, and became the signal, or the signator, of discovery.

Then when Leibniz died, then the forces of evil came back into play; then you had some people in society who would sustain the intention, but you have to think of the number of Presidents in the United States who were evil. A whole stream of Presidents of the United States were all evil! A whole bunch of them; and you saw that recurring again, as an era of evil.

And then Abraham Lincoln's intervention, with his backer and so forth. And what's happened is exactly that. Then you find that the people who are most important for the future of mankind are killed! Not fortuitously, but intentionally.

Why Einstein Was a Threat

And so therefore, these kinds of understandings are the kinds of things that enable people to really scrape together the information they need. But the point is, mankind is not located in the flesh as such; mankind is located in the creative powers of mankind. And it's those creative powers and the nature of those creative powers as a relative standard, which is the thing that defines the purpose of the existence of mankind.

Rogers: One thing you see is a defeating or rejection of sense-certainty, or this empiricist Cartesian view of the universe, a rejection which was expressed as maybe you could say, a continuity amongst all of these great figures.

LaRouche: Yes, it is, but it's in passing, because if these people die, and they don't have people who maintain the continuity of this legacy, then society collapses. And what happens is, you've got the killing of the Kennedy brothers, for example. What was the effect of the killing of the Kennedy brothers? Who did it? Why was it done? What was the effect? Where was the solution?

We tried to do it, with Reagan, we tried to do that. I was assigned to do that. And when Reagan was then shot, he was weakened,—that is, his ability to function and to control the society was weakened; he still had his own opinion and so forth. Matter of fact, the Bush family crowd tried to make a mockery of him, and he opened up his new speech that he was going to give, and he began a series of jokes: And the Bush people said, "uh-oh! Don't touch it! Don't touch it, that'll backfire!"

Unfortunately, that's what happened. So I got dumped just exactly for that reason; I was dumped precisely because I was continuing that purpose.

Sare: Well, they attempted to kill him; you were dumped; Indira Gandhi was assassinated, there were a series of efforts to prevent the development.

LaRouche: Absolutely. Her murder, by the British, coincided with putting me in prison. The same purpose. And the President was working with her. I had made the contact for establishing this standpoint of cooperation between the President and her. Shut down! And the history of India was turned down, because of the break that followed her assassination,—same thing.

There are similar aspects, in my direct knowledge which I know of, of just exactly this kind of thing.

Bill Roberts: Einstein's a good case of this, too, because you can see why Einstein was so brutally attacked if you understand his appreciation, for example, for Kepler. Because he knew exactly what Kepler was doing; he praised Kepler as knowing that a further understanding of the organization of the universe, had to be found in the mind, first; and then you find it in the universe.

But in order to get there, you have to painstakingly, get rid of, basically, all the crap; all the Aristotelian garbage that had been built up over hundreds and hundreds of years. So you can understand exactly why Einstein was seen as such a threat, why he was attacked, and why his leadership couldn't be allowed to be the current that people would follow in the United States and other places.

LaRouche: Yes. And that is what we have to,—as we assembled here, in this moment,—what we have to be concerned with. You have to see that there is no simple continuity, of human development; but that there are a succession of leaps, and that those leaps continue—just imagine that Kepler had lived, instead of dying when he did; dying of lack of nutrition essentially. And he was wandering around there on the field of battle, trying to play a role for his own family and for other purposes. And there was a discontinuity.

And between the death of Kepler and the rise of Leibniz, you see the gap. And the importance of that gap, the fact that it was a progressive process, and if you get into the details of Leibniz's development,—which has a whole history in itself, it's actually brilliant. But then, when there's no one to continue what Leibniz represented when Leibniz was dead! And the forces of evil were *delighted*! They were screaming around "is he dead yet? Is he dead yet?" And only when they were assured that he was actually dead, they triumphed! And that became the core of the Eighteenth Century.

Pearl Harbor and Today

Sare: One thing before we close today which I did want to ask, since you're the only one among us who was actually present and living when Pearl Harbor was bombed,—and that is today,—and I think that was a

From a fresco by Masaccio (1401-1428) in the Brancacci Chapel in Florence, a purported portrait of Filippo Brunelleschi.

break in a certain direction, if you have anything you'd like to say about that?

LaRouche: Well, absolutely! I think we had great generals, including one who dealt with the Pacific Ocean region, MacArthur. And what did they do with him? They bounced him out! He was the greatest military leader that we had at that time: They bounced him out. What happened as a result?

And this is how it works! And therefore you have to realize,—like the members in Congress,—what members of Congress are really evil clowns. Not because they're evil as such, by intention—though some are— but because they're stupid! And stupidity is a crime!

Deniston: Especially if you're in charge of a nation.

LaRouche: Yes. And this Obama thing is something which is a British thing. The whole thing, the whole problem that we're dealing with, *was* and *is* and *has been* the British system. The British system is the thing that has to be destroyed. And Obama's a key tool of the British system, so his career has to be destroyed, permanently! So nothing like him should ever come back again into the history of the United States. And that's what the problem is.

We have to understand what the problem is, and you have to understand it, because if you don't understand it, then you're not capable of dealing with the threats against humanity.

Deniston: And you look at Obama, and I think it's just worth emphasizing your demonstration of the validity of the method you're talking about now, because you didn't wait for popular opinion to go against Obama; you didn't wait for him to start droning innocent civilians; you knew that this was what the principle was, and you went after him, you led the fight against popular opinion. You were kicking the crap out of our own members and the general population on this war threat, years ago, when the popular opinion evidence wasn't there. That's been crucial in actually getting out front in leading the fight against this now. I mean, it was the winter of 2011-2012, that you were calling out the threat on this thermonuclear war under Obama's watch.

So it really is, I think, what you're saying about the role of individuals in actually creating an intervention, not just going with popular opinion...

LaRouche: Yeah. The absence of what we should have been a supply, or shall we say, a flow of discovery, and it's the flow of true discovery, as such—not, "I have discovered this"—but the fact of the *process* of discovering something new. You don't discover something as a *fait accompli*; you come to understand a revelation— "Oh! This is what I must do. This is the vacuum, I've got to deal with this vacuum; I've got to satisfy that vacuum," and that's how mankind progresses.

That's what Einstein did; just take his history of his discoveries, it worked exactly that way. He went with a series of events of discoveries. And each one he rejoiced in,—then he said, "well, that's not adequate, I've got to do this next."

And that's the way things work. But if you take the point, and you don't have a decent education system,— like the California education system, it's destructive! And if the pupil in the school system tries to open his mouth for an independent view or question, he could be bounced! In Manhattan, leading teachers in Manhattan are bounced, for this kind of reason!

And therefore, *that's* the thing we have to concentrate on, the general thing we have to deal with. Because we have the ability to stimulate progress; but then you've got the forces of evil, in the educational system, for example, in Wall Street and so forth. Garbage! Absolute garbage! Degeneration. And this is what destroys mankind. That's what frustrates mankind. And that's why it's important to kick what has to be kicked, and kick it far away from where it is.

Sare: All right. Well, that's a good challenge. [laughter] Is there anything else? I think we'll accept that as the challenge for the immediate future. So with that we'll sign off: Thank you for joining us, and stay tuned to larouchepac.com.

Zepp-LaRouche Addresses Japanese Business Leaders: World Land-Bridge To End War

by Jeffrey Steinberg

Dec. 4—Schiller Institute founder and chairwoman of the German political party Civil Rights Movement Solidarity Helga Zepp-LaRouche addressed two Tokyo events on Dec. 2, delivering a sharp message to 400 Japanese business leaders that the World Land-Bridge is the only way to end the tyranny of war and geopolitics and solve the ongoing Middle East crisis. In the morning, Mrs. Zepp-LaRouche addressed the eighth annual Asia Innovation Forum, attended by 300 young Japanese entrepreneurs and hosted by Nobuyuki Idei, former Chairman and CEO of the Sony Corporation and now the founder and CEO of Quantum Leaps, as well as the founder of the Asia Innovators' Initiative.

She gave a similar presentation later in the day to a smaller group of business leaders gathered at the Canon Institute for Global Studies. The text of her speech, with a sampling of the graphics she used, is included at the end of this article.

In evaluating the events, Mrs. LaRouche noted that they reflected the fact that there is a minority faction in Japan which realizes that the long-term, fundamental interest of their country is to avoid getting involved in a conflict with China, as it is being pushed to do by American warmongers, and instead link up with the World Land-Bridge and China's New Silk Road.

A Solution on a Higher Level

In her comprehensive presentation, Mrs. Zepp-LaRouche warned of the global pattern of regional wars that can easily lead to global catastrophe, including a new superpower conflict, and emphasized that the only way to change the course of events was by fundamentally changing the paradigms of thinking. What has to be applied is the method of Cardinal Nicholas of Cusa, dubbed *coincidentia oppositorium*, which calls for the individual to conceptualize a "one" as a solution to the "many" problems to be found on a lower level.

Zepp-LaRouche went through a detailed presentation on the World Land-Bridge, identifying the major

EIRNS/Jeffrey Steinberg

Presenters at the Dec. 2 Asia Innovation Forum. From left to right, moderator Daisuke Kotegawa; Helga Zepp-LaRouche; Paul Nogueira Batista, Jr; Vladimir Yakunin; and Dominique Strauss-Kahn.

global projects that can transform the world, citing Chinese President Xi Jinping's "One Belt, One Road" as the seed of a global renaissance. She spelled out the immediately available great projects, many of which had actually been supported by the Japanese Ministry of Industry and Technology in the 1970s and '80s.

She then developed the idea of mankind as a unique species capable of creating a future through creative discovery. She also highlighted the American System concepts of the first American Treasury Secretary Alexander Hamilton, and American System followers Henry and Mathew Carey, and detailed how those ideas spread around the globe in the Nineteenth Century, and were utilized in creating the modern nations of Germany and Japan under Chancellor Otto von Bismarck and the Meiji Restoration.

In fact, it is these ideas that are embodied in the World Land-Bridge/New Silk Road project now underway today.

The Panel

Mrs. Zepp-LaRouche was joined on the panel by former IMF Managing Director Dominique Strauss-Kahn; former head of the Russian Railways and co-founder of the Rhodes Dialogue of Civilizations, Vladimir Yakunin; and Paulo Nogueira Batista, Jr., the former Brazilian director of the IMF, who is now a Vice President of the New Development Bank, founded by the BRICS and headquartered in Shanghai. The panel was moderated by Daisuke Kotegawa, a former Japanese Ministry of Finance top official who was also Japan's IMF director at the time of the 2007-2009 financial crisis.

During his presentation, Dr. Yakunin strongly endorsed Mrs. Zepp-LaRouche's World Land-Bridge proposal, noting that Russia's Eurasian Development Corridors and China's One Belt, One Road policies were thoroughly compatible, and represented the "new paradigm" of thinking that is urgently needed to avoid wars brought on by the dying system of neo-liberalism. He emphasized that Presidents Putin and Xi were committed to Russian-Chinese cooperation to realize those Eurasian infrastructure links.

In his opening remarks of the panel, Strauss-Kahn detailed the ongoing crisis of the world financial system, and mentioned the possibility of a "perfect political storm" occurring in the near future. He acknowledged that the austerity policies now being applied were a fail-

EIRNA

EIR's Jeffrey Steinberg and Helga Zepp-LaRouche at the Canon Institute, Dec. 2, 2015.

ure and had to be replaced by a growth model, while admitting that there is no real support for a viable change in policy from within the dominant world financial institutions today.

The Canon Institute

In the afternoon, Mrs. Zepp-LaRouche addressed a separate event, sponsored by the Canon Institute for Global Studies, which was attended by 100 top executives of the major Japanese industrial corporations and financial institutions, as well as of the Japanese government's overseas investment agencies and funds. Moderator Kotegawa is the research director of this institute.

There were three speeches given at this event, followed by discussion. This author delivered a detailed picture of the real process of economic and social breakdown of the United States—a process largely covered up in the international media. An outline of that presentation follows the text of Mrs. Zepp-LaRouche's presentation on the World Land-Bridge as the only way to defeat the geopolitical drive to world war.

Then Nogueira Batista, who designed the new bank, gave an in-depth report on the progress of the BRICS New Development Bank and the plans to begin issuing development loans by April 2016. While insisting that the new institutions were not meant to replace the current financial architecture, he reviewed the history of the launching of the Bank by the BRICS countries as a response to the abject failure of the "Washington institutions"—the IMF and the World Bank—to reform in the wake of the 2008 financial collapse. He put special emphasis on the associated Contingent Reserve Arrangement founded by the BRICS, a $100 billion fund pledged to help reduce exchange volatility in trade and investment relations between member countries.

'The Need for Global Public Works: The New Silk Road Becomes the World Land-Bridge'

by Helga Zepp-LaRouche

Dear Ladies and Gentlemen,

The sheer number of explosive crises around the globe makes previous pre-world-war situations look calm by comparison. The recent downing of the Russian fighter jet by Turkey, which qualified American sources say Turkey would never have done without tacit support from the White House, and the subsequent support given by both President Obama and NATO to the Turkish action, demonstrate how close we are to the present, new Cold War becoming a hot war. This is underscored by the launch-on-warning-readiness of the nuclear arsenals of the United States and Russia, which have a decision time of mere minutes.

The fact that Russia and China correctly regard the U.S. Ballistic Missile System in Eastern Europe, and the Prompt Global Strike and Air Sea Battle doctrines, as First Strike doctrines directed against their nations, has already led to a new arms race. Trans-Atlantic military experts warn that the situation now is more dangerous than during the height of the Cold War, due to the lack of any codes of procedure or reliable emergency "red telephone" communication mechanism between the United States and Russia.

Aggravating this unthinkable danger is the overriding dynamic which arises from the United States' insistence that a unipolar world must be maintained, while,

FIGURE 1

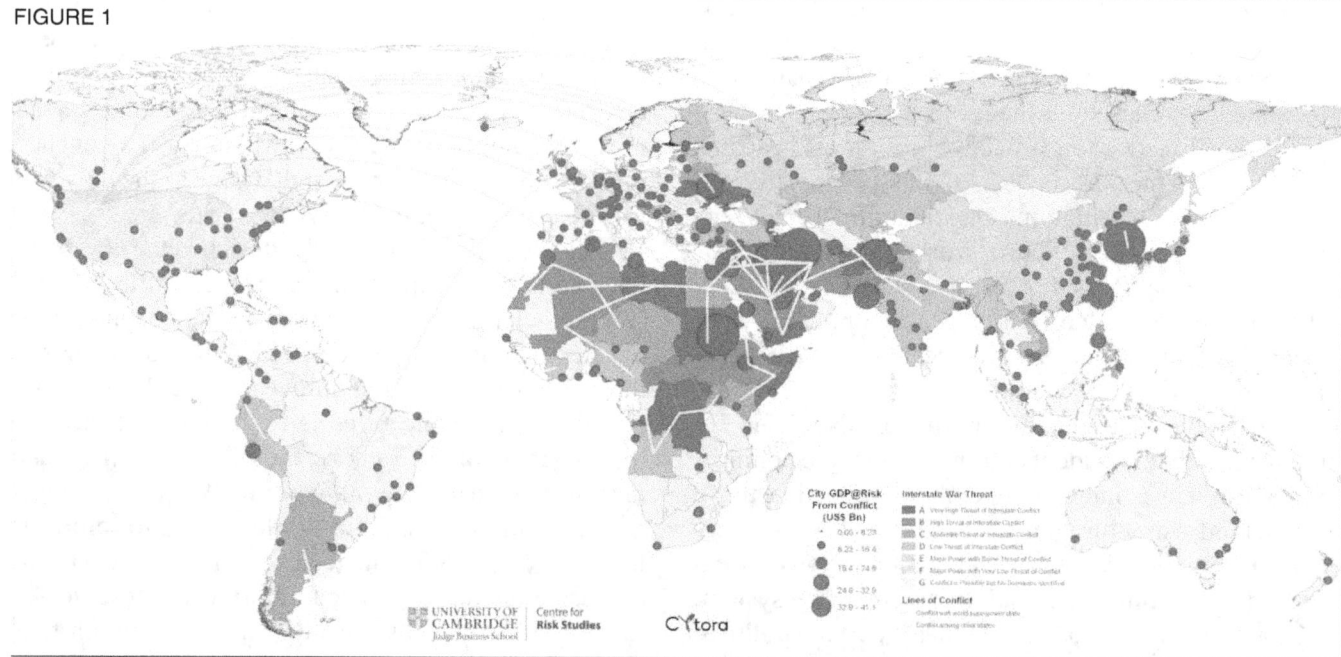

University of Cambridge/Centre for Risk Studies

A recent assessment of the danger of interstate conflict put together by Cambridge University.

FIGURE 2

Schiller Institute

The predictable result of not changing the current paradigm.

in fact, rising Asia, by its sheer weight, has already created a multi-polar world. The warnings of experts, such as former U.S. Joint Chiefs of Staff Chairman Gen. Martin Dempsey, that the West should not fall into the Thucydides Trap, seem to go unheard.

In addition, the crisis situation in Ukraine, the tensions in the South China Sea, and the Satanic degree of barbarism demonstrated by ISIS and Boko Haram, underline the mortal danger humanity is facing.

Equally threatening is the prospect of a new crash of the trans-Atlantic financial system, which would be more dramatic than the 2008 Lehman Brothers collapse, a crash which the central banks no longer have any viable instruments to cope with.

Do we have to be condemned to continue down this road, when all signs speak to the likelihood that these conflicts will escalate either to global chaos, or to a global thermonuclear war and the likely annihilation of the human species? Is the human species too stupid, indifferent, or degenerate to abandon these policies, even when their failure is already overwhelmingly clear?

'Coincidentia Oppositorum'

In the Fifteenth Century, the famous German philosopher Nicholas of Cusa stated that complex problems cannot be solved with a heterogeneous assortment of partial solutions; rather, one must find a solution on a higher level, where the contradictions of the lower level are resolved. He called that method of thinking the "coincidentia oppositorum," the thinking of the coinci-

dence of opposites. This is the idea that the One is of a higher order than the Many.

It is that method which must be used to define a new paradigm in the evolution of the human species today. And it is eminently possible to define a new paradigm which represents the true interest of all nations and all groupings.

Generally, people only become willing to even think about such new ideas when they realize that their underlying assumptions, which they have taken for granted for a long time, have been exposed as completely inadequate. And that is precisely the situation in which we find ourselves now around the globe.

This is most acutely true for Germany, where a qualitatively new debate is taking place in many circles abaout the need to reassess the strategic situation,—a debate guided by a growing perception that if the present policies are continued, the ultimate effect will be like a full-speed crash against a brick wall.

In particular, the refugee crisis has shattered the illu-

Nicholas of Cusa (1401-1464), on the left

A Syrian woman and her three young children after crossing from Turkey to the Greek island of Lesbos, Sept. 2015.

UNHCR

sion that any one country can be an island of stability, and that ongoing wars are far away. All of a sudden, there is a public discussion about the root causes of the refugee crisis, which is blowing apart the unity of the European Union (EU): causes such as the Anglo-American wars based on lies, the Saudi financing of terrorism, and Turkey buying oil from ISIS.

All of this is creating an openness in people's thinking to seeing the necessity for a dramatic change in policy! If terrorism is to be permanently eradicated and the refugee crisis overcome, operations against ISIS must take into account its decentralized structures in many countries. But military means are not sufficient: What is needed is real development!!!

It is urgent that a comprehensive reconstruction program for all of Southwest Asia and Africa be put on the top of the agenda. Only if young people, and especially the young men, have the perspective of a future,—including the possibility of raising a family, of becoming scientists, doctors, or architects,—can the environment for the recruitment of the jihadists be dried out.

All Will Benefit

Presently, the only realistic perspective for accomplishing such a goal is the extension of the policy of the New Silk Road into both the Near and Middle East, as well as into Africa. The outline for this approach is pre-

sented in the study *The New Silk Road becomes the World Land-Bridge*, which defines basic preconditions for a global reconstruction program.

Much of Southwest Asia has been "bombed back into the stone age," or was already a desert. A comprehensive infrastructure program for the entire region from Afghanistan to the Mediterranean, from the Caucasus to the Persian Gulf, must be put on the agenda. War must be declared against the deserts, by creating large amounts of new fresh water through the desalination of ocean water by means of nuclear energy, or ionization of moisture in the atmosphere. The latter would result in the creation of new rain patterns through the development of agriculture and reforestation.

It is necessary to build infrastructure corridors, with integrated high-speed train systems, highways, and waterways, in order to provide conditions for the location of industries and new cities.

All major neighboring countries of Southwest Asia have a fundamental security interest in participating in such an approach, and therefore must join forces in this project. This includes Russia, because of the close connection between ISIS and the Chechen terrorist networks, as well as the influx of heroin from Afghanistan into Russia; China, because of the connection of ISIS to the Uighurs; and India, since it has a Muslim population of 120 million people and has already had Wahhabi-Salafist-sponsored terror attacks in Mumbai and other places. Iran and Egypt, as well as Germany, France, Italy, and, clearly, in real terms, also the United States, have a fundamental interest in solving this problem.

Every nation and every region would benefit from the World Land-Bridge:

1. Japan: For Japan, participation in great projects of the World Land-Bridge would re-establish the tradition of the Meiji Restoration of Okubo Toshimichi and Okuma Shigenobu, whose policies were inspired by Alexander Hamilton and Friedrich List. These policies stem from the understanding that it is the development

FIGURE 3

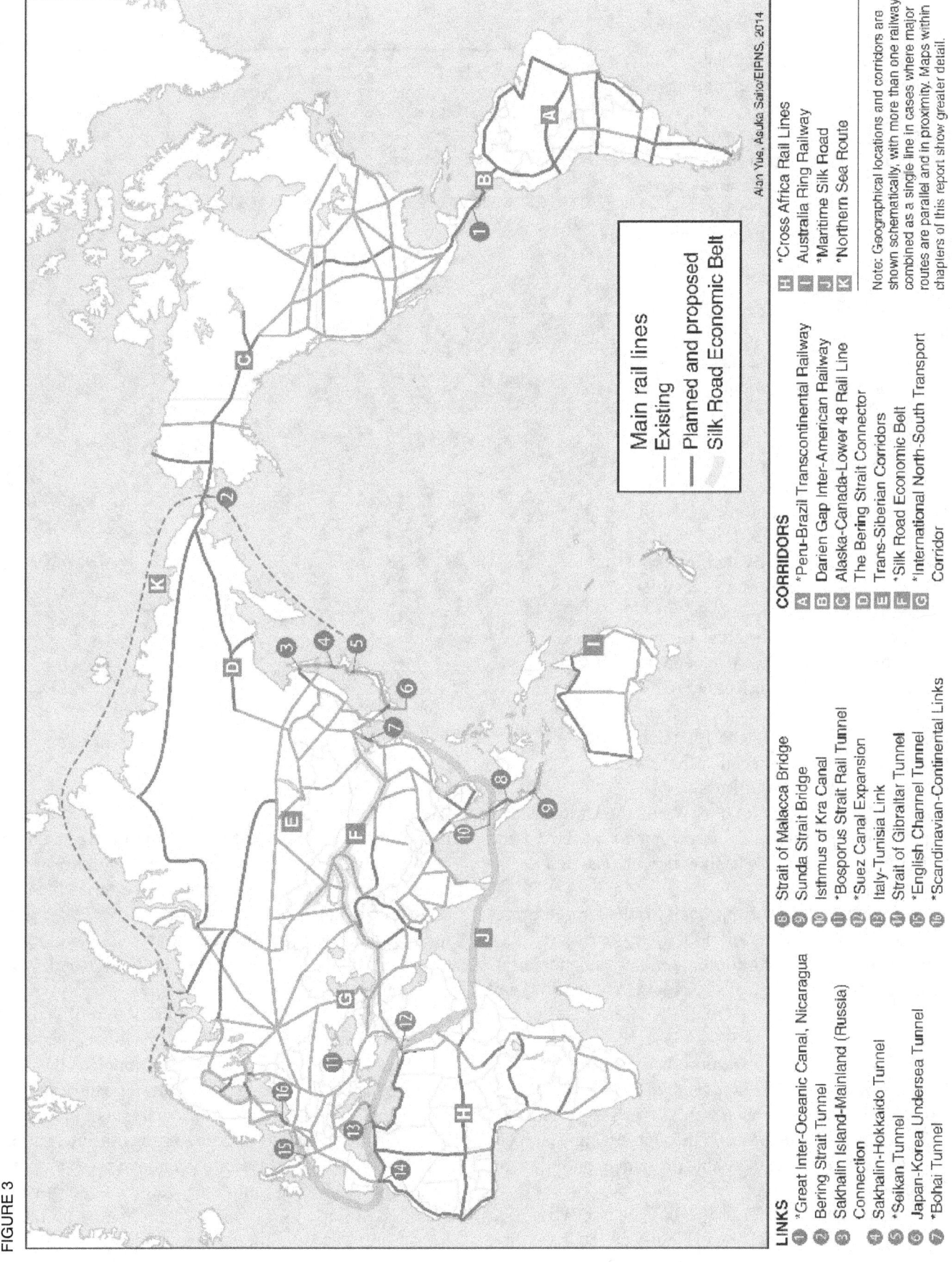

Alan Yue, Asuka Saito/EIRNS, 2014

Main rail lines
— Existing
— Planned and proposed
— Silk Road Economic Belt

LINKS
1. *Great Inter-Oceanic Canal, Nicaragua
2. Bering Strait Tunnel
3. Sakhalin Island-Mainland (Russia) Connection
4. Sakhalin-Hokkaido Tunnel
5. *Seikan Tunnel
6. Japan-Korea Undersea Tunnel
7. *Bohai Tunnel
8. Strait of Malacca Bridge
9. Sunda Strait Bridge
10. Isthmus of Kra Canal
11. *Bosporus Strait Rail Tunnel
12. *Suez Canal Expansion
13. Italy-Tunisia Link
14. Strait of Gibraltar Tunnel
15. *English Channel Tunnel
16. *Scandinavian-Continental Links

CORRIDORS
A. *Peru-Brazil Transcontinental Railway
B. Darien Gap Inter-American Railway
C. Alaska-Canada-Lower 48 Rail Line
D. The Bering Strait Connector
E. Trans-Siberian Corridors
F. *Silk Road Economic Belt
G. *International North-South Transport Corridor
H. *Cross Africa Rail Lines
I. Australia Ring Railway
J. *Maritime Silk Road
K. *Northern Sea Route

Note: Geographical locations and corridors are shown schematically, with more than one railway combined as a single line in cases where major routes are parallel and in proximity. Maps within chapters of this report show greater detail.

of the creativity of human labor, and the government's development of science and technology, which are the sources of wealth in society. This tradition was continued by the Japanese Ministry of International Trade and Industry (MITI) after the Second World War and by the Mitsubishi Global Infrastructure Fund, which worked on many of the projects which are part of the World Land-Bridge Program.

One of those projects, the Kra Canal, which will enable the increased flow of goods in the Pacific region, is again on the table. A second Panama canal is being built in Nicaragua by Chinese companies; the Mekong Delta complex is still urgent; the Transaqua-Lake Chad project has been reactivated by several African countries and a feasibility study is in progress.

The plan for building the Bering Strait tunnel has recently become more timely, given the Russian-Chinese collaboration on the "One Belt, One Road" policy and the Eurasian Economic Union, especially for Siberia and the Far East of Russia.

FIGURE 4

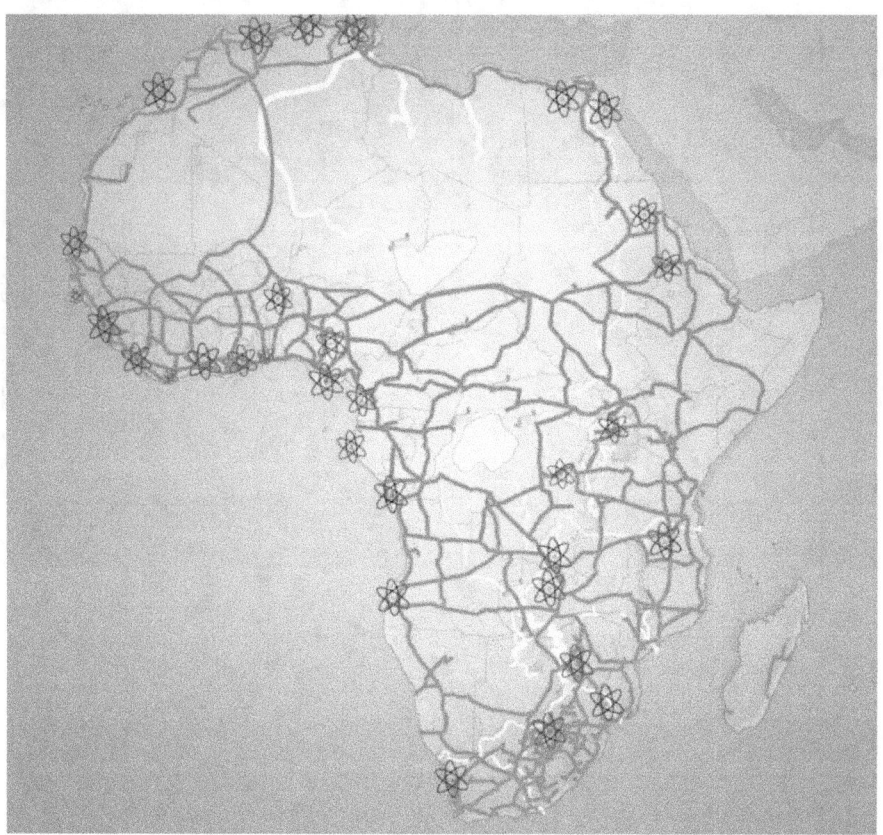

Schiller Institute

A schematic of a development plan for Africa, with new transport corridors and proposed nuclear energy plants.

2. United States: Not only would the United States benefit from joining in the development of Africa and Southwest Asia, but it is itself in urgent need of a reconstruction program.

The New Silk Road approach for the United States would mean the construction of a continental fast train system of 50,000 kilometers, new science cities in the South and West of the Rocky Mountains, and various programs for the creation of new weather patterns.

3. Ukraine: Collaboration between Europe, the Eurasian Economic Union, and the "One Belt, One Road" policy for the construction of infrastructure corridors could reunite Ukraine through creating an economic miracle instead of the present economic collapse.

4. Europe: All of Europe has an overwhelming backlog of infrastructure projects which have not been carried out because of a lack of investment. In Germany alone, this shortfall is an estimated two trillion euros. In 2012, the Schiller Institute presented a plan for a new economic miracle in Southern Europe, the Mediterranean, and Africa, as an alternative to the devastating austerity policy of the Troika. In light of the escalation of the refugee crisis, this development program, as an extension of the New Silk Road, would be a complete strategic game changer.

5. Africa: Because of the combination of wars and the denial of economic development by application of ecologist and monetarist ideologies, much of the continent, as in Southwest Asia, resembles Hell on Earth, rather than being countries its occupants enjoy living in. The announcement and beginnings of international cooperation to realize a comprehensive development plan for the African continent, would send a powerful message of hope to millions of people now on the run from war, terrorism, hunger, and epidemics.

FIGURE 5

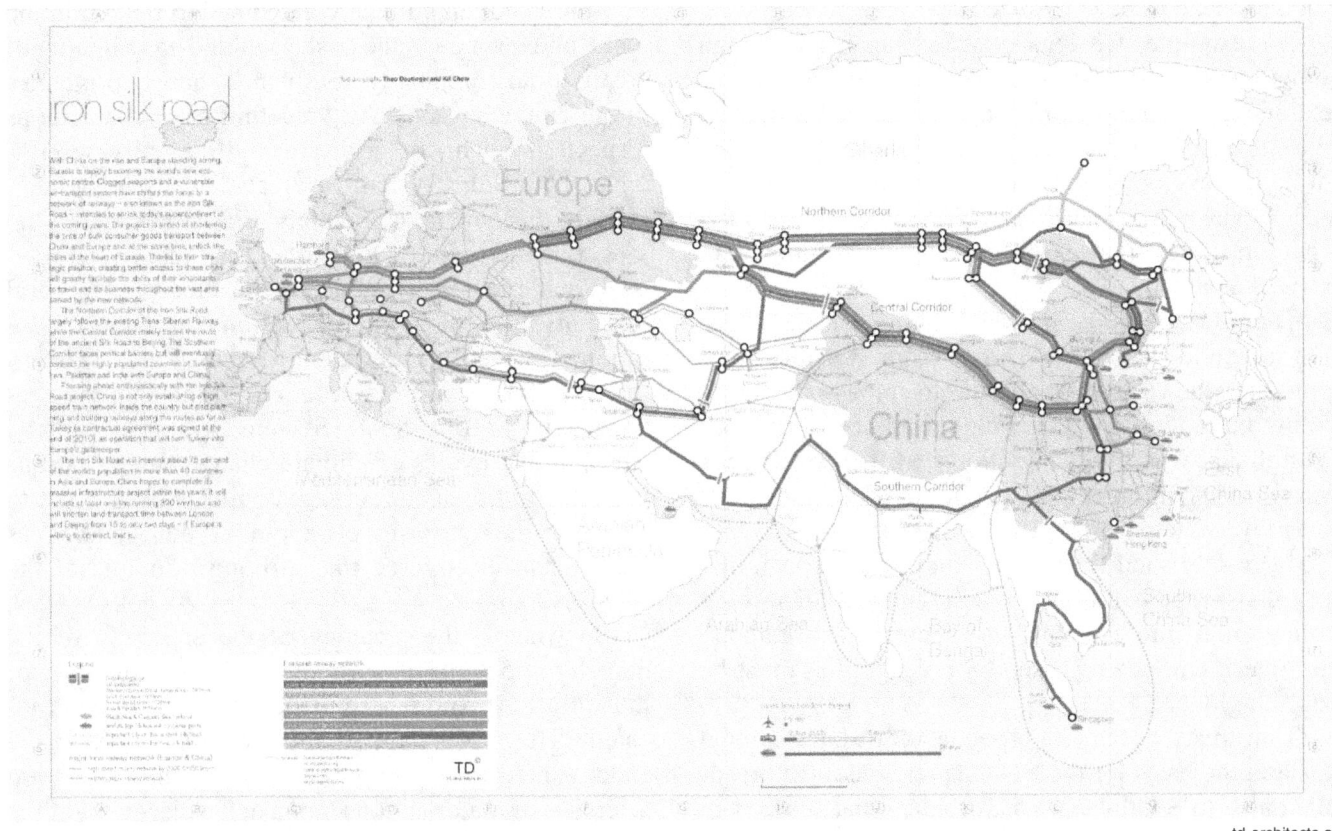

A schematic of the Iron Silk Road, drawn in June 2011.

A New Paradigm: The World Land-Bridge

The World Land-Bridge, as a concrete basis for a peaceful world order for the Twenty-first Century, however, requires a new paradigm of thinking. The alleged legitimacy of geopolitics—the idea that one nation or a group of nations has a self-interest which they can pursue against the interests of another group of nations, by military means if necessary, is, in the age of thermonuclear weapons, obviously outdated—unless one wants to risk the annihilation of the entire human species.

The assumption that it would be possible to "win" a "limited" nuclear war based on a First Strike Doctrine is ludicrous, and has been refuted by impeccable military analysts. Its advocates should be prosecuted in compliance with the principles established by the post-World War II Nuremberg Tribunal.

Mankind will only be able to survive the present crisis threatening its existence, if we can make the qualitative jump to defining the common interests of man-kind as the point of reference. The question "Where should mankind as a whole be in 100 years, or 1,000 years from now, and beyond" must guide decision-making. The World Land-Bridge will not only provide for the infrastructural development of the landlocked areas of all continents, but it also will define the next phase of the evolution of the human species by extending the idea of infrastructure into space.

If either (in the best case) an immediate emergency summit of the UN General Assembly, or otherwise an early G20 summit or meeting of some of the most future-oriented leaders of the world (in government positions as well as present and former representatives of the scientific, industrial, diplomatic, and cultural communities), would put such a World Marshall Plan, a World Land-Bridge, on the table as a peace plan for the Twenty-first Century, there would suddenly be a perspective of hope for the world.

The idea of the World Land-Bridge elevates the discussion to a higher level of reason, creating a higher geometry in which all the historical and ethnic conflicts can disappear, or be neutralized.

For example, tensions between Japan and China sometimes seem insurmountable; however, in the context of collaboration with India, Russia, and the nations of Southeast Asia and Europe in this proposed "Peace through Development Plan," the mutual benefits of such a win-win perspective would represent an overwhelming incentive to shape the future, rather than relive the past.

There are obvious differences between the situation now and that of the Thirty Years War, but what motivated the various war parties to come to the negotiating table then and conclude the famous Treaty of Westphalia, was the recognition that if this religious war were to continue, there would soon be nobody left to enjoy a victory. The Peace of Westphalia Treaty (1648) established for the first time in European history that peace can only be maintained if all foreign policy takes into account "the interest of the other," and that it can not be based on revenge, but must be based on love.

That treaty became the foundation of international law and the basis for the UN Charter, and must be applied also to Southwest Asia, despite what some with opposing opinions think.

Unfortunately, respect for international law has vanished. The highest authority of the UN, the UN Security Council, has ceased functioning since the regime-change operation was run against Muammar Qaddafi.

International law must, therefore, be re-established and further developed. The principle which must be agreed upon, and which must underlie all considerations, like a preamble, is that of the common aims of mankind—that no nation's interests are legitimate, if they do not coincide with the interest of all of humanity, with respect to its present and future existence.

The principles of the UN Charter remain valid, but this proposed preamble must take into account a higher lawfulness, which is referred to differently in different cultures: In European philosophy it is called "Natural Law"; in Asian philosophy, "Cosmic Order." It expresses the idea that mankind as a whole can only survive in the physical universe at large if the political and economic practices on planet Earth are being brought into coherence with the laws governing our universe.

Mankind, the Creative Species

Man is not an animal, condemned to remain in the mode of existence of the past. Mankind has a quality of creativity to continually discover the deeper principles of our Universe, constantly redefining our character as a species. When Kepler discovered the unifying principle of our Solar System, he created the basis for mankind to become a completely different species, no longer bound to Earth, but part of the Solar System.

When Einstein discovered the theory of general relativity, he created the foundations for man's exploration of space. It is now clear from the Earth's history that there are defining influences of the changing relationship of our Solar System with the Galaxy, which effect cycles of climate change and variations in the evolutionary processes of life. We have yet to discover the unifying principle of our Galaxy, as Kepler had discovered the unifying principle of the Solar System.

So what is the meaning of the creativity of the human mind, since it is an integral part of the laws of the Universe? And where is the future of mankind located? The next phase of the work in space, in the Galaxy and beyond, requires collaboration among top scientists of major nations to make the discovery of the laws of our Universe a new scientific frontier. If mankind is going to continue to exist, we have to develop our powers to discover aspects of the universal laws of the Universe which are completely unknown today, just as the existence of Helium 3 on the Moon was unknown during Kepler's time.

There is no closed Earth system, but life on Earth is defined by the lawfulness of the Solar System's interaction with the Galaxy; and we still have to discover the unifying principle of all the billions of galaxies. The meaning of life is the advancement of mankind's ability to master the challenges of discovery of the pathway to the next discovery, the one necessary for mankind to continue its existence in the millions and billions of years ahead. So far, we have only deciphered the shadows of the principle.

It is therefore an existential requirement to return to the principles of physical economy and real science, and to eliminate monetarism. We have to restore the knowledge of the history of the theoretical foundations of the various industrial revolutions, which has been almost eliminated from the economics textbooks of western universities.

FIGURE 6

Man's destiny in the Universe. Above right and lower left, the International Space Station; below right, Liu Yang, China's first female astronaut.

Schiller Institute

The Essential Principles

It is a fact that the industrial revolutions in the United States, as well as in Germany, Japan, and Russia and, more recently, the Chinese economic miracle, were all based on the principles of physical economy of Gottfried Leibniz, Friedrich List, American System economists Mathew and Henry C. Carey, and Russian Count Sergey Witte.

The Meiji Restoration succeeded in rapidly transforming Japan into a major world economic power, thanks to the theories of Alexander Hamilton and Friedrich List. (Erasmus Smith, a very close collaborator of Lincoln's economic adviser Henry Carey, was sent by the Ulysses Grant Administration as an official economic adviser to the Meiji Restauration.)

The rapid transformation of Germany from a feudal state into an economic powerhouse, was based entirely on the tradition of Friedrich List, and on Otto von Bismarck's encounter with the economic model of Henry C. Carey, mediated by, among others, Wilhelm von Kardorff, then head of the German industrial association. Germany would have not become an industrial nation, but for Bismarck's conversion from a follower of free market theories into a protagonist of the protectionist policies of List and Carey.

The Chinese economic miracle of the recent 30 years, especially the policies of the New Silk Road and the alternative banking system—embodied in the AIIB, the New Development Bank, and the Silk Road and the Maritime Silk Road Funds—follow the same traditions. The 5th World Congress of China Studies in the Spring 2013 in Shanghai, and the 2014 List conference in Reutlingen, Germany, emphatically made the point that the German economist List is the most popular economic theoretician in China, not Adam Smith.

List regarded the development of the productive powers of labor and industrial capacities as more important than statistical wealth; he would be an adamant critic of today's asset-driven economies. In the paper he submitted to a contest sponsored by the French Academy of Sciences in 1837, he developed a vision for the future role of transport systems, a "space and time economy," which contains ideas still valid for the World Land-Bridge today.

He considered the continuous perfection of transport and communication systems to be the precondition for the progress of humanity, enabling human beings to increasingly realize all the potentials nature gave to human beings. The more that talented people could exchange their ideas and collaborate in all areas of endeavor, the greater progress could be made in all areas of knowledge, and science and the arts would be would be inspired and spread to all sectors and disciplines.

Anticipating our present jet age, List said that the easier it becomes for human beings to move from place to place, the more mankind would be able to save time and compress space, and the resulting development and efficiency of man's greater powers would increase and utilize the material riches of nature more effectively for his purposes.

The impact of this characteristic of what List called the "Space and Time Economy" would be shown in the increased wealth of nations, which would develop advanced transport and communication systems, even if their "natural environment" was unfavorable. The high degree of speed, regularity, and cost-efficiency of transport would facilitate new levels of the development of the mental and material productive forces.

FIGURE 7

Schiller Institute

The American System economists: From top left, clockwise—American Henry C. Carey, Russian Count Sergey Witte, German Gottfried Leibniz, and German Friedrich List.

In an almost prophetic forecast, List saw this development leading towards uniting all nations in one humanity, in a "Republic of the planet," based on the "economy of Mankind."

The realization of the World Land-Bridge, proceeding from the standpoint of the common aims of mankind, is eminently feasible in the near term. But it must be accompanied by a dialogue among the high levels of the different cultures of the world. For many Asian countries that means Confucius; for India, the Gupta period and Indian Renaissance; for Russia, Alexander Pushkin and Vladimir Vernadsky; for Italy, the Italian Renaissance; for Germany, the Classics in music and poetry. Out of knowledge of each others' culture, love and admiration will grow.

This is the only way that representatives of different cultures can access their fundamental identity as members of the only creative species known in the Universe,—a species which, so far, is only in its childhood, but which can and must become the immortal species.

Implementing this vision requires individuals today who are guided by a passionate love for humanity.

'The Real State of the U.S. Economy'

This is an outline of the Dec. 2 presentation by EIR *Intelligence Director Jeffrey Steinberg at the Canon Institute in Tokyo, based on his notes. A transcript is not yet available.*

If you follow the mainstream U.S. media, or the pronouncements of the Obama Administration on the state of the U.S. economy, you are being fed a totally false picture, with claims of a gradual recovery and almost robust job creation. Nothing could be further from the truth, and I will give you a brief picture of what has actually happened to the U.S. economy, under the Obama Administration and the preceding Bush Administration.

Every month, the Labor Department's Bureau of Labor Statistics (BLS) provides an in-depth statistical report on employment. Mainstream media and the Obama Administration spokesmen cherry-pick a small fraction of the data and present a rosy picture of declining unemployment. But a more careful look at the very same data paints a very different, devastating picture of Depression-level unemployment and underemployment.

Seven Truths the Obama People Hide

1. The BLS hides the real unemployment and underemployment picture. Ninety-four million working age (16-65) Americans are not counted in the labor force. Working-age unemployment is more than double the official figure. Forty percent of the employed workforce earns under $15,000 per year, which is a minimum-wage full-time salary. Twenty-three million employed Americans earn under $5,000 per year.

2. The collapse in earning power and wages is related to the changing character of the American economy. Only 12.8% of the employed labor force is engaged in goods-producing activity, which is mining, construction, and manufacturing; 8.2% of the total workforce is engaged in manufacturing; and 79.9% is employed in the service sector, which includes 15% who are employed by the Federal, state, and local governments. While not all service jobs are a net loss to the real economy, it is still a fact that almost 80% of those employed are part of overhead costs, and are not directly involved in producing anything that can be held, used, or sold.

Ten percent of U.S. manufacturing is defense production. Since 2001, 42,400 factories have been shut down. Ninety thousand additional factories are in jeopardy of

SaraRemington.blogspot.com

Collapsing industry: Detroit's Fisher Body 21 and Packard Car Plant today. In 1960 a thriving auto industry gave Detroit the highest per capita income in the country.

being shut down in the coming decade. While some manufacturing job loss can be attributed to technological advances, including robotics, new generation computerized machine tools, and the like, the factory shutdown data makes clear that some of the loss of manufacturing jobs is not based on such advances. The 2005 shutdown of much of the U.S. Midwest auto sector is the clearest example of this factor.

Another true measure of the manufacturing decline is the dramatic collapse in the U.S. machine tool sector, where there was a 23% decline in output from 1998 to 2009. During the same period, China's machine-tool output increased by 714%. Today the United States accounts for only 5.1% of global machine-tool production. There was a period, not so long ago, when the United States, Germany, and Japan were the giants of the machine tool sector, worldwide. That is no longer the case.

Marc A. Hermann/MTA New York City

Infrastructure collapse: A water main break in April 2015 floods the New York City subway.

3. **The nation's infrastructure is in horrible shape.** The American Society of Civil Engineers produces an Infrastructure Report Card every four years (the latest report card was in 2013). Overall, the ASCE gave the U.S.A. a "D" (an improvement over the "D-" of four years prior). Between 2015 and 2020, to maintain infrastructure at a stable level would require a $3.6 trillion investment. The ASCE projects that there will only be $2 trillion spent, deepening the deficit. This does not even take into account the need for improvements, just maintenance.

4. **The Too-Big-To-Fail banks are 40% bigger, and are more exposed now to a looming derivatives blowout, than they were at the time of the September 2008 Lehman Brothers collapse.** The Richmond Federal Reserve Bank reports

that another bailout like 2008, would cost taxpayers $26.5 trillion, more than the 2008-2010 bailout. Thomas Hoenig, Vice Chairman of the Federal Deposit Insurance Corporation (FDIC), says that unless there is a return to Glass-Steagall, a new and bigger blowout is inevitable.

As the result of the quantitative easing (QE) bailout

FIGURE 1
Ready for the next blowout

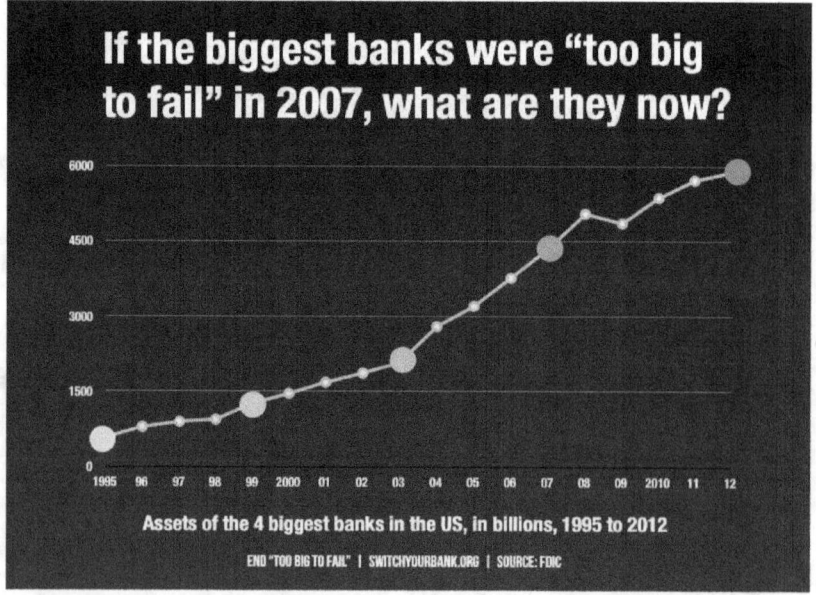

If the biggest banks were "too big to fail" in 2007, what are they now?

Assets of the 4 biggest banks in the US, in billions, 1995 to 2012

END "TOO BIG TO FAIL" | SWITCHYOURBANK.ORG | SOURCE: FDIC

program, the Fed now holds $5.2 trillion in assets, over half of which are troubled. Just prior to the 2008 crash, the Fed's assets portfolio was $800 million.

The Fed cannot do another QE without triggering a hyperinflationary blowout, and the Fed does not dare sell off any of its portfolio for fear of triggering a collapse.

The Fed's zero interest rate policy, now in its seventh year, has robbed retirees and those saving for retirement, of interest earnings, forcing them to either enter into more risky stock market investments, or lose interest earnings. This means they either live off of savings or face serious austerity choices. One analyst estimates that the zero interest rates have robbed retirees of $10 trillion dollars, a fact which has also seriously impacted the consumer economy.

5. Commercial banks are over-exposed to junk debt, especially in the energy sector, which is largely tied to the cycle of bankruptcies and defaults occurring in the capital-intensive fracking industry, due to the collapse of the oil price globally.

For example: The *Energy Intelligence Briefing* of Dec. 1 cited an S&P report that 77% of oil exploration and production (E&P) companies have junk debt ratings, out of 153 such companies which have ratings at all. Furthermore, banks have cut their credit to the oil/oil service sector by only 10% in 2015 so far. So it's about to happen. Their debt service share of operating cash flow is now over 85%. Forbes forecasts that the next significant oil companies to fail will be Goodrich Petroleum (GDP), Swift Energy (SFY), Energy XXI (EXXI), and Halcón Resources (HK), among others. These companies have all lost more than 90% of their market value since 2014.

6. Social consequences: The Centers for Disease Control declared a heroin epidemic in August 2015, with the greatest growth in heroin addiction among households earning $50,000 a year or more—middle class income. Among those households, heroin abuse rose by 60% in the last four years where data is available. A recent Princeton study found that middle age death rates have also skyrocketed since 2001. While every other advanced sector nation has experienced a continuing decline in the death rate, the United States has gone into a death spiral, largely driven by the psychological fallout of a collapsing economy: drug abuse, depression, suicide, despair.

FIGURE 2
Drug poisonings lead the death surge

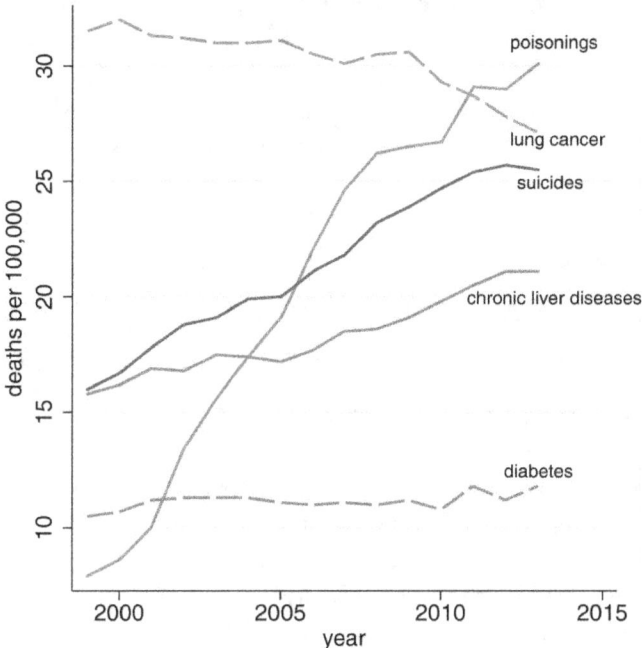

Proceedings of the National Academy of Sciences

Wages of despair: The astronomical rise in mortality among white non-Hispanics aged 45-54, documented the a study by Princeton professors Anne Case and Angus Deaton, is led by poisonings, which consists heavily of drugs.

7. Youth are hardest hit by the economic consequences of the policies of the last two administrations. In 2013, there were 30 states out of 50 where youth unemployment and underemployment was greater than 30%. In five states—Nevada, Illinois, Mississippi, California and North Carolina—the rate was over 40%.

What Can Be Done

The solutions are at hand:

• Reinstate Glass-Steagall banking separation, which will wipe out taxpayer bail-out/bail-in obligations.

• Launch Federal capital investment in vital infrastructure, including high-speed rail and water management.

• Revive NASA.

This means the United States becoming fully engaged with the 'One Belt, One Road' World Land-Bridge project. Establish either a Hamiltonian National Bank or an equivalent, such as the Reconstruction Finance Corporation (RFC), which FDR used to generate the rebuilding of the U.S. economy from the last great depression.

Every Day Counts In Today's Showdown To Save Civilization

Europe Is Asking: Is there Opposition to World War III Within the United States…Or Is it All Over?

by Robert Ingraham

I. Fear and Self-feeding Panic

The news from Europe is sobering. Current reports starkly portray an escalating process of social disintegration and desperation, as the effects of the Anglo-American military escalation against Russia continue to unfold. The recent dramatic worsening of the military conflict in and around Syria has raised the specter of general warfare into the consciousness of many thinking Europeans. Increasingly, the possibility of World War III is being discussed more and more openly. At the same time, the Obama-created refugee crisis has brought more than one million refugees to Europe, and more than 500,000 to Germany alone during the last two years. In August of this year, the German government announced that it expected to receive 800,000 applications for political asylum during 2015. The social tensions, the economic strains and the fear of new terrorist attacks, such as what occurred in Paris on November 13th, are driving Europe into a crisis, the likes of which have not been seen since 1945.

There are courageous leaders in Europe who recognize the danger of this current directionality, and more than a few of them are taking steps to sabotage the current British-American war drive against Russia. However, it is clear to most that any European-based opposition can not possibly succeed as long as a madman occupies the White House. The recent decisions by Obama to deploy U.S. military forces into both Iraq and Syria, without the approval of either the United States Congress or the governments of those two nations, combined with the U.S. and British use of Turkey as their proxy in escalating the military conflict with Russia,—all of this presents European leaders with a very pessimistic scenario as to what to expect from the United States in the days ahead. The Obama-authorized drone killings have further driven home the point that Obama is a cold-blooded killer who will not be deterred from his current course of action by traditional diplomatic means.

For many in Europe, the growing likelihood of general war is beginning to appear unstoppable, and the fear generated by that analysis is bolstered by a view of

creative commons/Johan Viirok

Barack Obama speaking in NATO member Estonia, in September 2014.

the U.S. political situation as monolithic, one in which any real U.S.-based opposition to Obama seems feeble at best, if not near non-existent. Under these conditions many in Europe see no alternative but to submit to the blackmail and pressures emanating from the White House. Many in Europe are asking: "Is there anyone in the United States willing and capable of stopping the present insane policy emanating from Obama?"

II. LaRouche: A True Strategy For Victory

In a recent discussion with associates, after reviewing the current catastrophic world situation and the escalation toward world war, Lyndon LaRouche posed the following challenge:

> How do you stop it, that's the point. How do you stop it? How do you stop the current course of history? Because everything, every problem of mankind, is the failure to stop the bad history which is in the making....
> And that's my nightmare concern.

In truth, there is growing opposition—some of it courageous—to the Obama war drive within the United States, but, if one applies the necessary yardstick as demanded by LaRouche, almost all of the statements and actions taken so far in opposition to Obama fall far short of what is needed, and needed now. Most of the criticisms and warnings that have so far been uttered by American elected officials and other public figures are far too timid, far too cowardly, and simply represent a re-arranging of the deck chairs on the Titanic as the ship sinks. There is great fear and cultural degeneration throughout every layer of American society. Something greater, something historic is required if humanity is to successfully overcome this current test of its worthiness. In discussing the moral qualities needed to win the present desperate battle, Lyndon LaRouche had the following to say to a group of his associates on November 28th:

> The problem is simply one of courage. But it's not a matter of formal courage, it's a matter of understanding what the issues of life for mankind and in nations represent. And, therefore, if you know what the facts are, and you have

knowledge of the evidence—and I have a certain amount of knowledge of these matters—you simply say, "We're going to win that war."

Now, that's not just a simple declaration, that we are going to go out there and wave our arms, and so forth, and win this war. We're going to have to understand exactly what this war means, and what the results would be if we caved in to the enemy. And therefore, if you cannot eliminate the enemy, defeat him, then you're not going to have anything. So therefore, you have to mobilize yourselves, in order to motivate a larger population to recognize that what you're doing is right and essential. There's never been much of anything else in known history, the history of warfare, and history of struggle in general. That's been the truth.

Now we have hoped, we have hoped and hoped almost futilely, that we could bring about what we call peace. Now peace is not quiet. It's not quietness. Peace is the progress of mankind. And let me emphasize one thing that I emphasize repeatedly, which most people tend not to attach themselves to. Mankind's greatest prospect lies in people who have died. It lies there because they were better at science and society than anyone else. And what they did is, their very existence gave mankind the means to bring mankind into a higher level.

Now, for example, one of the greatest sources of corruption is the belief in being personally practical. People who think that life is based on being practical, are cowards, and because they are cowards, they are also idiots. The purpose of mankind has always been, as the case of Kepler, for example, or as the case of Nicholas of Cusa, models of this case, that if you stand for that, and you can convey the meaning of that, which is the future of mankind, a future which mankind has not heretofore achieved. And that is the highest goal of human achievement.

Now, people are going to die. Human people, historically, always die; except for a few people who made it so far, a handful of people. Everybody else dies. The question is under what condition do they die, and under what conditions do their circles of life represent? Do you represent, in your society, a power of creativity for the future of mankind, which mankind has never achieved before? And it's only when you get to that point that you understand that principle, that you find yourself equipped with the ability to make the argument, and sustain the argument which has to be done.

This is not a sacrifice, because you're going to lose your life anyway. You don't live, you don't have a full life. Anybody who's 100 years of age, or even my age, that's not really the issue. The issue is what the future of mankind represents. And the future of mankind means, what can you do, for example, in schools? What can you do in educational systems, to make the population that you are supposedly educating, achieve a level of achievement in knowledge and effectiveness which mankind has never experienced before? Isn't that the great achievement?

LaRouche PAC

LaRouche PAC organizing in Manhattan.

When we look at the history of mankind, we study the history of mankind, as I've studied the history of mankind at some length in the course of my life, it's the people who create a *new* opportunity, a more advanced opportunity, a corrected opportunity, and it's those people who mean something.

People who work to get by and pass tests, and get rewards, they are not very important. The only very important people are those whose actions by themselves are a contribution to the improvement of humanity in general. And that's what we all have to concentrate on. That's the only thing that's really redeeming, in terms of the history of mankind. Can you produce an achievement for mankind as a whole which has never been achieved on that level before? And if you have a devotion to that goal, and understand the goal, then you are very powerful. Because the history has shown that it's human achievement, of that type, which has been the motive force by which mankind has survived and achieved....

III. Lyndon LaRouche's Manhattan Project

Actual leadership is required if Barack Obama is to be forced from office and the threat of global war averted. That leadership exists in the United States. It is courageous, and it is committed to victory. It is to be found in the Manhattan Project, the organizing initiative launched by Lyndon LaRouche in October of 2014.

Over the recent weeks, volunteers and organizers from that Project have unleashed an intervention into the cultural and political life of Manhattan with the uncompromising demand that Obama must be removed from office NOW if world war is to be prevented. Every component of the Manhattan-based establishment, from academia, to elected officials, to the diplomatic community is being confronted on a daily basis with the reality of Obama's war drive, confronted in a manner where there is no place for them to hide or to avoid the truth. People are being forced to face the consequences that it is only their own folly in tolerating Obama that allows this deadly progression toward war to escalate.

Growing numbers of New Yorkers are being recruited into this fight. The success in growing this movement has been precisely because it is not a "practical" political movement. The Project-affiliated Community Chorus has been at the heart of aiding individuals to transform their own self-conception and to locate their activity as world-historical women and men acting on the future, acting to interrupt the deadly trajectory of present history. As in Lyndon LaRouche's recent discussions of Filippo Brunelleschi, the question of a truly human identity has been at the heart of the choral work of the Project.

If *Executive Intelligence Review* were to report in detail on all of the day-to-day political organizing of the Manhattan Project, the entirety of this current issue would be taken up by such reports. It is sufficient to say that this organizing is extensive; it is relentless; and it is bold. Only two examples of that organizing will be reported here, and those to provide tactical examples for any patriot, anywhere in the nation, who desires to act now:

On December 1st, in Manhattan's upper west side, a team of Manhattan Project organizers confronted the anti-Putin chess grandmaster Garry Kasparov at a book-signing ceremony at the local Barnes and Noble. Kasparov was there to promote his latest screed *"Winter is Coming: Why Putin and the Other Enemies of Freedom Must Be Stopped."* Kasparov is well known as a propagandist who equates Vladimir Putin with Josef Stalin and Adolph Hitler. The Manhattan Project organizers denounced Kasparov as a liar and as a pawn of the Obama war drive. *LaRouche PAC* leaflets, including "Put Obama Under Lock and Key to Avert Nuclear War," and "Obama Wades Further into the Sea of Blood," were distributed to the assembled crowd, amid a polarization of the audience and heated discussions on the reality that Obama is leading us into World War III.

On the very same day, another team of Manhattan Project organizers intervened into an event at New York University, sponsored by Indonesian experts who were gathered to discuss the hidden history of the massacres and mass slaughter which took place in Indonesia in 1965-1966. Three organizers intervened with separate briefings on the involvement of Obama's step-father Lolo Soetero in that mass genocide, and the way in which this family heritage has shaped Barack Obama's murderous personality. In the midst of freak-outs and great consternation from the podium, the Manhattan Project organizers forcefully made the urgent point, as

demanded by Lyndon LaRouche, that Obama's character as a murderer and the use of murder by Obama as a policy, from kill lists to drones, to the threat of nuclear war, to Obama's own self-description as someone who found that he was good at killing—that this was all linked to the role of Obama's step-father in one of the biggest massacres in recent history. The point was driven home that in the present, perilous, global environment, it is insanity to have the power of the Presidency in the hands of someone with these kinds of psychological problems, and that clearly Obama must be removed from office.

IV. The Still Too-cowardly Institutional Opposition to Obama

During the last 30 days, opposition from among U.S. elected officials and other public figures to the Obama war drive has surfaced publicly within the United States in a way which is unprecedented when compared to the slavish subservience to Obama that has characterized most U.S. establishment leaders over the last six years. Some of this opposition, such as Congresswoman Tulsi Gabbard's challenge to Defense Secretary Ashton Carter at a hearing of the House Armed Services Committee on December 1, has been very courageous. Other criticisms of Obama, such as a recent speech by former Secretary of Defense William Perry and separate recent writings by *Washington Post* columnists Richard Cohen and Dana Milbank, have been very weak. Most of the anti-Obama interventions lie somewhere between those two poles. A few examples will provide a flavor of this activity:

On November 27th, Bruce Blair, a former nuclear launch officer and a co-founder of Global Zero, posted an article on the *Politico* website titled "Could US-Russia Tensions go Nuclear?" In the article, Blair warns that the current state of relations between the United States and Russia is at a hair-trigger for nuclear war. Specifically, Blair points to dramatic changes in military deployments and procedures that have been implemented over the last two years, since January of 2014, which have dramatically lowered the threshold for the launching of all-out war. Blair describes the current "launch-on-warning" insanity which has been forced on both Russia and the United States by the strategic doctrine of the Obama administration. As of this

Department of Defense/Glenn Fawcett

Former Secretary of Defense William Perry on Dec. 3 warned of an exacerbated "risk of nuclear war" with Russia. Here, he's shown speaking at the Pentagon in March 2015.

moment, according to Blair, if either President Obama or President Putin are presented with a report of a "possible" attack on their nation, they would only have 2-6 minutes to decide on whether or not to launch a full strategic nuclear attack. In reality, as other analysts have shown, given the delays and real time difficulties involved in passing along such a warning, the actual time for the head of state to decide to unleash Armageddon would be 30 to 60 seconds… or less.

On November 29th, Germany's *Der Spiegel* magazine interviewed U.S. Lieutenant General (Ret.) Michael Flynn, the former head of the Defense Intelligence Agency, who was fired by Obama, and who then publicly accused Obama of knowingly pursuing policies which created and spread ISIS. In the interview, General Flynn laid the blame for the current spread of international terrorism squarely at the door of the White House, including both its previous occupant, George W. Bush, and current resident, Barack Obama, as the responsible parties for the creation of ISIS and the current crisis in the Mediterranean. In the interview the following exchange took place:

Spiegel: There would be no ISIS if the Ameri-

cans had not invaded Baghdad in 2003. Do you regret…

Flynn: Yes, absolutely.
Spiegel: …the Iraq War?
Flynn: That was a colossal mistake.

In a December 2nd interview with *Russia Today*, Senator Richard Black of Virginia identified Obama's pawn Turkey as the most loyal ally that ISIS has in the Middle East, and he described in detail the supplying and arming of ISIS through routes that pass through the Turkish-Syrian border, the same routes used to finance ISIS by means of oil tankers traveling from ISIS-controlled areas into Turkey.

In addition to those cited in the preceding paragraphs, other public figures have come forth in opposition to current Obama policy, including speeches or interviews by former U.S. Senator Mike Gravel, former Vice Chairman of the Joint Chiefs of Staff Gen. James Cartwright, former Secretary of Defense Chuck Hagel, Republican Congressman Dana Rohrabacher, and Republican Presidential candidates Ted Cruz and Mike Huckabee. All of these individuals have struck at some aspect of the Obama madness, ranging from Obama's support for the ISIS terrorists to the danger that Obama's military escalation against Russia is leading us to the brink of world war.

Additionally, there are the continuing efforts of former Senator Bob Graham, Congressman Walter Jones, and their allies to speak out and demand the release of the full 28 pages which were excised from the official report of the Joint Congressional Inquiry into the 9/11 attacks, pages which will implicate the Presidencies of both George W. Bush and Barack Obama in covering up the role of Saudi Arabia in carrying out that attack.

Tulsi Gabbard

During a House Armed Services Committee hearing on December 1st, Representative Tulsi Gabbard (D-HI) confronted Defense Secretary Ashton Carter on the looming danger of a devastating thermonuclear war with Russia as a consequence of Barack Obama's policies in Syria.[1] During the course of this exchange, Con-

---

1. For a full report on this exchange, see: http://larouchepac.com/20151202/rep-gabbard-warns-nuclear-war-us-war-overthrow-assad

Rep. Tulsi Gabbard, during her Dec. 1 confrontation with Secretary of Defense Ashton Carter.

gresswoman Gabbard peppered Carter with a series of questions, questions which made him increasingly defensive as they progressed.

Gabbard began by stating, "Since our policy to overthrow the Syrian government of Assad has brought us, essentially, into a direct head-to-head conflict with Russia, I have some important questions along this line. How many nuclear warheads does Russia have aimed at the U.S., and how many does the U.S. have aimed at Russia?"

After a non-response from Carter, Gabbard continued, "And it would be correct to say that both of our countries have the capacity to launch these nuclear weapons within minutes?"

Gabbard then proceeded to discuss the patrolling of the Turkey-Syria border by U.S. F-15s, and how this military deployment could have as its only purpose the targeting of Russian planes. Despite repeated attempts by Defense Secretary Carter to both change the subject and blatantly lie, Gabbard persisted, stating the obvious truth that the current U.S. military actions in and around Syria can only lead to head-to-head conflict, i.e., a shooting war, with Russia.

This personal "interruption" by Representative Gabbard is the first time that any sitting member of Congress, speaking within the Capital building, has identified that the recent military decisions taken by the Obama White House are propelling the us to the brink of world war. It is an heroic act, more so because other members of Congress, governed by their own fears of Obama, have been cowed into silence.

V. The Necessary Method

In recent discussions, both public and private, Lyndon LaRouche has stressed the importance of learning the true lessons of history. Not the "facts;" not the names, dates, *et al.* Rather, the true revolutionary way in which real human history is made.

In these discussions, LaRouche has repeatedly returned to two themes—the first being the concept of "placement," and the second being the personage of Filippo Brunelleschi. This present article is not the place for an in-depth examination of either of those themes.[2] Nevertheless, it is important to state here that when LaRouche raises the issue of "placement," he is not discussing it as a mere musical methodology; nor, when LaRouche discusses Brunelleschi is he simply raising the issue of Brunelleschi's architectural or engineering skills. Rather, LaRouche is proposing a challenge to every individual to discover the actual nature of the human identity, and thus to discover the way whereby our current historical trajectory—our real-life tragedy—might be changed.

In a recent discussion, LaRouche stated that he now fears the collapse of history, the end of history; that we are at the edge of the extermination of the human species. He asked, what do we have to do?

How do you stop it, that's the point. How do you stop it? How do you stop the current course of history? Because everything, every problem of mankind is the failure to stop the bad history which is in the making. And that's where most of our own people are screwed up. They say, what's a practical solution to this problem? And if you're not influencing the *future* thinking of the population, you ain't doing nothing. You're not doing anything important. The idea that, you know, history will tell you what the future is,—history does *not* tell you what the future is! Mankind's development determines what the future is.

And Brunelleschi is a good example of this. His work is an excellent model, because he was

2. For a more in-depth presentation by Lyndon LaRouche on the significance of Brunelleschi, see: https://larouchepac.com/20151207/lpac-policy-committee-show-december-7-2015

a leading figure in a crucial period of the Renaissance. His work was absolutely magnificent. And that's where you have to *generate* the future, not react against it: generate the future.

A deductive notion of mankind's future is for idiots. You have to create the future, and you don't derive the future from the past. You free mankind *of* the past. You don't learn from the past, you learn to get out of it.

And that's exactly what is not happening since the beginning of the Twentieth Century, with Bertrand Russell's operation in particular,—what's the direction in which mankind is going? Down! *Down!*

These are the problems, and the fact is that we're not intelligent enough, and we haven't learned from history. I spent most of my activity in learning history, ancient history, all kinds of history. And you're looking for the change, which *is* history. And it's not something that happened to you; it's something that you pushed, and made happen.

And if you don't have that sense of pushing, to make something happen which must be made to be caused to happen, then you're a failure, and your opinions are a failure.[3]

An egregious example which shows a failure to rise to the level of identity that LaRouche states is required, a failure to overthrow the normal "go along to get along" mind-set of the American establishment, can be seen in a recent article, one critical of Obama's anti-Russia policy, authored by Stephen Cohen and his wife Katrina vanden Heuvel. Cohen is a well-known author, professor, and Russia expert. Vanden Heuvel is the publisher and editor of *Nation* magazine. Together, on December 2nd, they published a piece titled "Coalition or Cold War with Russia?" After detailing the dangers inherent in the current situation, the "deterioration" of U.S.-Russia relations, and the failures of current American foreign policy, the two authors offer no options and no alternatives to the current disaster. They end the piece by issuing an appeal (plea) to Obama to "transcend (his) own political biography."

This article is particularly cowardly because Stephen Cohen is a long-time critic of U.S. policy toward Russia, having warned, specifically during the Bush-Cheney years, that U.S. policy was leading to military confrontation with Russia. Cohen is well aware that the danger of war with Russia is far greater today than at any time during the Bush Presidency, yet we see this milquetoast piece of garbage urging "transcendence" upon Obama, rather than identifying Obama as the killer he is, and demanding his removal from office.

Compare the cowardly inadequate actions of Cohen and many others to what LaRouche stated at a recent meeting:

> Look, we're on the edge of the extermination of the human species; don't worry about who's talking about what, what kind of weapons and so forth. It doesn't make any damn difference. In less than 20 minutes, you're dead; and your death will have been announced and reported throughout the planet. How long does it take for a full-scale thermonuclear blast against a great nation? And what will remain as a result of that blast? Possibly, absolutely nothing; except waste.
>
> And therefore, what do we have to do? Well, the simple thing is we say, "If we get rid of Obama, if we throw him out of office, this is a new story." And people say they're going to negotiate with Obama, that is real stupidity. If you're negotiating with Obama, you're a traitor to mankind.
>
> I don't think our people really understand how deadly the present moment is. I mean, you have to take a measurement of what is the charge that is going to launch the war? How much? How many? What's Obama doing? What's the effect of his existence?

In another presentation, this one before a recent Manhattan Town Hall Meeting, LaRouche stated that the current challenge all comes down to personal responsibility, personal courage:

> And that's how it works. And I don't worry about anybody except me. I'm responsible for me, and what I can contribute to any around me. That's it! And I don't have any other standard. I appreciate people who achieve things. I'm happy when I meet it. I'm happy when they are intelli-

3. More on this theme can be found at: https://larouchepac.com/20151127/you-have-very- little-time-change-your-thinking

gent, and I'm miserable when they are not. But I try to get over that.

So the point is, in this point, every individual human being, in the final analysis, is totally responsible to themselves for the future of mankind. And when people understand that, as I do, that's the best. You have to have a standard of your own life, which is defined for the benefit for all mankind. And you will not compromise that for *anything*. And otherwise, if don't do that, you become a failure. And I don't intend to be a failure. They may kill me, but I won't be a failure.

The True Lesson from History

If one is to understand how to change history, one must understand how this has been done in the past. This requires an understanding of what history is not. History is not a chronology. History is not a linear progression of events. History is not evolutionary. In one sense, the history of the human species has been one of degeneration and cultural decay, degenerations which have been *stopped* and *reversed* by revolutionary *interruptions*, interruptions which have often saved humanity from catastrophe, and at times resulted in a profound upsurge in human culture and the human identity, as seen in the European Renaissance.

It has been those interruptions, those interventions, which have had long-lasting effects on human society, and it is very useful to ponder the reality that the founding of the American Republic and what has been positive in American society down to the present day has all been a product of those still existing, if weakening over time, reverberations from that Renaissance of more than a half millennium ago.

In American history, the greatest insight into this scientific principle of creative human intervention is to be found in the personage of Alexander Hamilton. What is crucial in understanding the issue involved is not the simple details of Hamilton's program, but the concept of the human identity and human creativity which inhabits his life's work. Hamilton was able to elevate a bunch of rag-tag colonies to something historic, something profoundly greater than any of the competing parts. Everything good in American history flows from Hamilton's courage and from this intervention. Later, other individuals in their own way acted to defend and

Founding Father Alexander Hamilton. One of his mottos, taken from Demosthenes, was: "As a general marches at the head of his troops, so ought wise politicians if I dare use the expression, march at the head of affairs; insomuch that they ought not to await the event, to know what measures to take; but the measures which they have taken, ought to produce the event."

promulgate this idea, a few with great success. Abraham Lincoln and Franklin Roosevelt, in particular, rose above the practical and political concerns of their time to save and revive the universal mission of the American Republic. Much of this has now been lost. For example, the reverence with which most American's once held Lincoln's poetic Gettysburg Address is now almost faded from memory.

As LaRouche has insisted, we as a species have oftentimes in the past tolerated long periods of decay. The current worsening degeneracy of the Trans-Atlantic community threatens mankind with not simply a catastrophe but with actual human extinction. A new interruption, a new creative human intervention is required. Yet this absolutely can not be achieved through "practical" means, nor if one is held back by fear to "go along to get along." Furthermore, although boldness and courage are absolute necessities for victory, the change needed now requires a more profound change in one's own sense of personal identity. Before trying to change anyone else, you have to change yourself.

Obama's Bought-and-Paid-For Agent

by Dean Andromidas

Dec. 8—In the early hours of November 24 a Turkish F16 jet fighter shot down a Russian Su-24 along the Syrian-Turkish border, making Turkey the first NATO country to have shot down a Russian warplane since the founding of the military alliance more that six decades ago. The idea that Turkey itself could have made such a decision that could have led to a major confrontation between the world's most powerful nuclear powers as a full member of the integrated military alliance, is too absurd to even consider.

There can be no other conclusion than that the decision was made in consultation with President Barack Obama. This should surprise no one because Turkish President Recep Tayyip Erdogan has been a full partner of Obama and his British imperial masters in the launching of not just a Thirty-Years-War policy in Southwest Asia, but a policy that will lead, if not stopped, to a thermonuclear confrontation between the United States and Russia that will devastate this planet.

The shooting-down of the Russian warplane was yet another insanely dangerous and provocative attempt to stop President Vladimir Putin's initiative to put together an international alliance, with the door wide open for cooperation with the United States, to destroy the Islamic State and other extremists that have been financed and supported by the so-called Sunni Alliance, i.e. Saudi Arabia, Qatar, the Gulf States, and Turkey, at the behest of their British masters.

Calling it a "stab in the back," Putin said it all in his first response, where he charged that Turkey has been buying oil pumped out of Syrian oil fields by the Islamic State on an "industrial scale." He declared:

> This explains the significant funding the terrorists are receiving. Now they (Turkey) are stabbing us in the back by hitting our planes that are fighting terrorism. This is happening despite the agreement we have signed with our American partners to prevent air incidents, and, as you know, Turkey is among those who are supposed to be fighting terrorism within the American coalition.
>
> If ISIS is making so much money—we are talking about tens or maybe even hundreds of millions, possibly billions of dollars—in oil

President Obama's first overseas trip as President took him to the UK, Strasbourg, Prague, and Ankara, Turkey. Here he addresses the Turkish Grand National Assembly on April 6, 2009.

trade—and they are supported by the armed forces of an entire state, it is clear why they are being so daring and impudent, why they are killing people in such gruesome ways, why they are committing terrorist attacks all over the world, including in the heart of Europe.

Do they wish to make NATO serve ISIS? I know that every state has its regional interests, and we always respect those. However, we will never turn a blind eye to such crimes as the one that was committed today.

Vadim Savitsky, Vadim Grishankin

The panel at the Dec. 2 media briefing on ISIS-Turkey oil smuggling, held by the Russian National Centre for State Defense Control.

On December 2 Putin kept his promise and a panel of top Russian General Staff Officers gave a powerful briefing to the media detailing Turkey's role in this illegal oil trade. (See documentation)

Erdogan: Obama's Full Partner in Genocide

Make no mistake, Erdogan is just a front man for Obama and the British. Erdogan represents the pro-Muslim Brotherhood faction in the Turkish Islamist political movement. The partnership started when Obama, during his first overseas state visit, went to Turkey in April 2009, and extolled the great historic partnership of the two countries. That trip was soon followed by Obama's trip to Saudi Arabia and Egypt in June 2009. In August of 2010 Obama signed Presidential Directive 11 calling for a study on how the United States should collaborate with the Muslim Brotherhood as "progressive and moderate Islamists."

This "collaboration" was, in fact, to carry out the policy of "regime change" that led directly to the overthrow of the Libyan government of Muammar Qaddafi, the launching of war against the Bashar al-Assad government of Syria, and the backing of the Muslim Brotherhood government of Mohamed Morsi in Egypt. These bloody operations were all carried out by the "Sunni Alliance."

Erdogan was an ideal choice for Obama to pair with. His ruling Justice and Development Party, allegedly a "moderate Islamic" party, held an absolute majority in the Turkish Parliament supposedly based on "democratizing" Turkey, and taming its military which had led military governments, one in the 1960s, and the other in the 1980s. Then-foreign minister, now Prime Minister, Ahmed Davutoglu had his "zero problems" policy with neighboring countries, including Syria.

But after joining Obama and the British policy of launching the plot to overthrow Assad, Erdogan began to show his true Muslim Brotherhood colors. Despite warnings from the Turkish opposition and saner elements of his own party, Erdogan threw his support behind the British policy to overthrow Assad by means of deploying an army of Sunni terrorist mercenaries drawn from all over the Arab world, Russia, and Central Asia, an army which has now morphed into the Islamic State.

When Muslim Brotherhood leader Mohamed Morsi became president of Egypt, Erdogan threw his full support behind him. When the Egyptian people removed Morsi from the Presidency (after the latter tried to bring Egypt into the war against Assad), Erdogan broke relations with Egypt and denounced Egyptian President Abdel Fattah al-Sisi as a "dictator." This too was under the orders of Obama, who has refused to fully back al-Sisi's presidency. Obama was a full supporter of Morsi and the Muslim Brotherhood's takeover of the most populous and politically important Muslim country in the Middle East. Shortly after Morsi took power in 2012, Obama extended an invitation to him for an official visit, only to cancel it when it became too hot an issue during the U.S. presidential election campaign.

Logistics for Terror

For more than three years Turkey has been the major logistics base for all the anti-Assad terror groups operating in Syria, including the Free Syrian Army, the al-Nusra Front, and the Islamic State. Thousands of Islamic mercenaries transit through Turkey, after arriving at Istanbul airport, and are allowed to make an unhindered passage across the Syrian border. Anti-Assad fighters freely cross the border for 'R-and-R' inside Turkey, and are even given medical care in Turkish hospitals. Several of the Paris terrorists and suicide bombers made these crossings back and forth for training in Syria to fight Assad.

This activity has not come without a price for the Turkish people as well. Not only is Turkey flooded with over two million Syrian refugees, who are literally being pushed out into the Mediterranean to Europe in Erdogan's campaign to blackmail the Europeans into supporting him, but violence and terror has overflowed into Turkey itself.

Support for the Syrian terrorist opposition ran counter to every historic tenet of Turkish foreign policy not to get sucked into Middle East intrigues and wars. Sane Turkish policy-makers knew that it would blow back into Turkey, which it did. Turkey, especially in the regions along the border it shares with Syria, has the same mosaic of religious groups, Muslim sects, and ethnic minorities as in Syria. In fact, the cross-border populations are closely related to one another with extended families living on both sides of the border. The launching of sectarian war led by so-called "Sunnis" has destabilized Turkey itself.

The Syrian war has sparked once again a conflict with the Turkish Kurdish population, which is located in the border region and accounts for more then 25% of the Turkish population. A so-called peace process aimed at ending the insurgency led by the Kurdish Workers Party (PKK) collapsed. On the other side of the border, the Syrian Kurdish Democratic Union Party (PYD) continues to fight against the Islamic State. Under Erdogan's orders, the Turkish army and security forces have been attacking both the PKK and the Syrian PYD.

While Turkish security forces are being killed

Davutoglu and The Muslim Brotherhood

Dec. 7—A leading strategic analyst in Malaysia who has known Turkey's Prime Minister Ahmet Davutoglu personally for a long time, told *EIR* that Davutoglu has been a Muslim Brotherhood asset for many years, as has President Recep Tayyip Erdogan. He said that in a meeting he had with Davutoglu in 2011, Davutoglu remarked that Iran, a traditional target of the Brotherhood, was becoming a serious problem; that for the first time in 1,000 years Iran was attempting to restore the old Persian Empire; and thus it had to be countered. Davutoglu also told him that President Bashar al-Assad in Syria was suppressing the Muslim Brotherhood and also had to be countered—long before the current uprising got started.

Davutoglu also intervened in Malaysian politics during the meeting of the G20 last month in Turkey, complaining to Malaysian Prime Minister Najib Razak about the conviction of Anwar Ibrahim, who has been a long-time representative of the Muslim Brotherhood in Malaysia (as well as an agent of Al Gore and Paul Wolfowitz in the destabilization of that country).

The source said he himself has been attacked by the friends of Turkey and the Brotherhood in Malaysia and elsewhere, because they are unhappy with his writings attacking Turkey's war provocations on behalf of the British and Obama.

every day, the Islamic State (IS) has been attacking the Turkish-Kurdish and other Turkish minorities with terror attacks inside Turkey itself. The most devastating attack Oct. 10, when two IS suicide bombers blew themselves up in front of the main railway station in the Turkish capital of Ankara during an election rally of the Kurdish Peoples' Democratic Party (HDP). More than 100 people were killed.

Erdogan's Caliphate of Corruption and Fear

After more than a decade in power, first as Prime Minister and now as President, Erdogan has developed delusions of establishing

Wikimedia Commons

Turkish President Erdogan's new Presidential compound in Ankara, Turkey.

a new Ottoman Caliphate. He has already abandoned Turkey's old presidential residence which was good enough for Ataturk, the Turkish Republic's great founder, for a 1,000 room palace modeled after an Ottoman palace; it cost no less than $600 million. He receives official guests with a presidential honor guard dressed up in historic costumes worn by Ottoman soldiers over the past centuries. His state visitors get a photo-op of themselves sitting with the "great leader" on golden decorated thrones.

More important is the fact that Erdogan has transformed the Turkish Presidency, which by the Turkish constitution is traditionally ceremonial, into an executive position by placing his personal protégé, Ahmed Davutoglu, as prime minister. Now that his party has once again won an absolute majority in the Parliament, Erdogan hopes to change the constitution and become officially an Executive President, if not a new sultan.

Nonetheless, Erdogan's new caliphate is nothing but a sham based on corruption and fear, in which he rakes in billions of dollars as chief facilitator for the wars that are raging in the region. It is an empire of massive smuggling, graft, and corruption maintained by authoritarian rule.

Erdogan controls this corrupt apparatus through his family. His son Balil sits on the board of the education foundation Türkiye Gençlik ve Egitime Hizmet Vakfi (TÜRGEV) which, according to Turkish media sources,

serves as a conduit for illegal payments.

According to *The Verge* news website, Balil is a major shareholder of BMZ Group Denizcilik ve Insaat Sanayi Anonim Sirketi, a marine transportation company which transports IS oil.

Erdogan's son-in-law Berat Albayrak has just been named energy minister in the new government. He was head of Çalik Holding, a conglomerate that controls pipelines and other energy infrastructure.

In December 2013 the Financial Crimes and Battle Against Criminal Incomes department of the Istanbul Security Directory detained 47 officials from various ministries as well as the sons of the minister of interior, minister of economy, and minister of environment. They were accused of taking bribes from two Iranian businessman, Reza Zarrab and his controller, the Iranian businessman Babak Zanjani. The latter is now sitting in an Iranian prison for high crimes, including fraud against the Iranian government and running a massive money-laundering operation.

Press reports have also implicated Erdogan's son Balil, who was said to have channeled illegal payments through one of the Islamic charities he controls.

In this stew of corruption surfaced Sheik Yasin al-Qadi, a Saudi "businessman" who had been put on the United Nations Sanctions list for his connections to the al-Qaeda leader, the late Osama Bin Laden. Erdogan himself at a public event called Yasin his good friend.

Yasin is said to serve as a conduit for billions of dollars of Saudi money to be invested in Turkey. Much of this money has gone into huge real estate projects in Istanbul, which has been Erdogan's personal stronghold since the days he was mayor of the city.

Erdogan reacted to charges against him with his customary rage, and had the prosecutors dismissed. He then proceeded to purge no fewer than 350 senior police officers, mostly from the anti-terrorist squads. He charged that the whole case was a plot by the followers of Fethullah Gulen, the head of a moderate Islamic community who has been in exile living in Pennsylvania for decades, to overthrow the government. Members of Gulen's movement, which is said to own the Turkish daily *Today's Zaman*, were in fact original supporters of the AKP, but broke with the party's policy of joining the Sunni Alliance.

Money and Weapons Flows

No sooner was this investigation crushed than a few months later, in January 2014, Turkish gendarmes, acting on an intelligence tip, stopped several trucks *en route* to Syria. According to press reports, they found they were filled with weapons and ammunition obviously headed for anti-Assad terrorists. Sitting next to the drivers were agents of the MIT, the intelligence service attached to the Prime Minister's office.

Erdogan again acted in rage, declaring the trucks were carrying humanitarian aid to Syrian Turkmen. He then ordered the gendarmes arrested, including the general officers and the prosecutor, charging them with a plot to overthrow the government and other wild charges. The affair led to yet another nation-wide purge of the security services.

The case surfaced again last month in the Turkish media when *Cumhuriyet*, one of Turkey's oldest dailies, published copies of documents presented to the court concerning the case, which detailed the amount of ammunition and weapons found on the trucks. In response, the daily's two editors were arrested and charged with espionage. They are currently sitting in prison.

These cases are only the tip of a huge iceberg of corruption which has seen tens of billions of dollars flow into Turkey. The money not only goes to support the fighting in Syria—that has led to 350,000 Syrian deaths and up to 10 million refugees,—but has lined the pockets of AKP officials and Erdogan himself.

The fact that billions of dollars have entered Turkey annually as "unregistered capital inflow," i.e. black money, has been documented in the leading Turkish daily, *Hurriyet*. The latter linked a rise in the inflow to funding of the AKP election campaign held only a few weeks ago where the AKP once again, contrary to all the polls, received an absolute majority.

Hurriyet showed that while the economy this year has been totally flat, the balance of payments deficit miraculously decreased. In 2014 the current account deficit was $42 billion. For the first nine months of this year it is only $25 billion. This drop to $25 billion came from $8 billion from known legitimate sources, $4 billion dollars from reserves, and the rest from "net error and omission" or "unregistered capital inflow." *Hurriyet* reported that this latter category is understood as "money laundering and foreign currency coming from the crime economy."

This "unregistered capital inflow," twice that of the same period last year, is said to be $13.44 billion. This only accounts for illegal transfers from outside the country and not the billions made on smuggling to and from Syria, which includes oil from IS and Turkish manufactured weapons and ammunition in the other direction.

The Turkish population itself suffers greatly from Erdogan's rule. The country is split down the middle. Half the population supports the AKP's rule by corruption and patronage. But the other half, comprising the republican current and ethnic religious minorities such as the Kurds, have been unable to mount an effective unified opposition that can unseat the AKP from power.

Nonetheless if Obama falls, Erdogan will soon follow.

RUSSIAN GENERALS

Russia Exposes Turkish-IS Oil Trade

Dec. 8—As promised by Putin, the Russian government and top-level military of Russia's General Staff on December 2 gave an extensive briefing to media on this illegal, "industrial-sized" operation through which

The panel at the Dec. 2 media briefing on ISIS-Turkey oil smuggling, held by the Russian National Centre for State Defense Control.

Vadim Savitsky, Vadim Grishankin

Turkey—most especially President Recep Tayyip Erdogan and his family—finances the Islamic State (ISIS), by purchasing the oil ISIS has stolen from Syria and Iraq. Deputy Defense Minister Anatoly Antonov, Lt. Gen. Sergei Rudskoy, Chief of the Main Operational directorate of the General Staff, and Lt. Gen. Mikhail Mizintsev, Chief of the National Center for State Defense Control, used satellite and reconnaissance photos, videos, and maps to demonstrate the extent of Turkey's "business" operations with the Islamic terrorists.

Spelling out the magnitude of the illegal operation, Gen. Rudskoy reported that, in total, it involves 8,500 trucks transporting up to 200,000 tons of oil daily, with most of the trucks entering Turkish territory from Iraq. In the two months that Russian air forces have been in Syria, he continued, they have destroyed 32 oil production facilities, 11 refineries and 23 oil pumping stations, plus a total of 1,080 tanker trucks. This has reduced the illegal oil turnover by almost 50%, and reduced illegal oil revenues from $3 million per day to $1.5 million per day.

But terrorists continue to receive financial resources, he warned, as well as weapons, ammunition, and other supplies for their activities

"Certain nations, primarily Turkey," Gen. Rudskoy said, "are directly involved in the Islamic State's large-scale business project, thereby aiding the terrorists. The General Staff of the Russian Federation Armed Forces has irrefutable evidence of Turkey's involvement based on aerial and space reconnaissance data." Deputy Defense Minister Antonov specified that President Erdogan, his family, and the country's "senior political leadership" were guilty of facilitating the purchase of oil from ISIS. In the West, he said, "no one has asked questions about the fact that the Turkish President's son heads one of the biggest energy companies, or that his son-in-law has been appointed Energy minister. What a marvelous family business!"

Lt. Gen. Mizintsev provided further detail on a flow of militants, munitions, and automobile hardware "coming from Turkey," which have provided key re-inforcements to ISIS and Jabhat al-Nusra.

Gen. Rudskoy presented the bulk of the very detailed report on the main transportation routes into Turkey used by the jihadis. The many maps, videos, and satellite images he used showed convoys of vehicles freely crossing the Turkish border, from Syrian territory controlled by al-Nusra and ISIS. "These vehicles are not checked at the Turkish side," he said, and there are hundreds of such vehicles. The Turkish ports of Dortyol and Iskenderun possess special mooring places for tankers; oil is loaded onto vessels and sent to oil-processing facilities outside Turkey. Rudskoy detailed locations of other oil-extraction operations, such as the region near Deir ez-Zor, under ISIS control, where large concentrations of tanker trucks can be seen waiting for shipments.

He pointedly explained that, "as there are no strikes by the U.S.-led coalition" on any of these convoys, the Defense Ministry will post on its website the "coordinates of active concentration areas with tanker trucks," for other nations to use. "The Russian aviation group will continue performing tasks concerning liquidating oil infrastructure facilities of the ISIS terrorist organization in the Syrian Arab Republic. The Russian Defense Ministry also encourages the coalition colleagues [to take] such action," Gen. Rudskoy stated.

There Is No Global 'Climate Danger'

Dec. 7—*American scientist Thomas Wysmuller denounces COP21 and the plot against the developing countries.*

NASA meteorologist and member of the Johnson Space Center Climate Group (ret.) Tom Wysmuller was interviewed in New York by Celestin Ngoa Balla for the weekly Cameroon newspaper Journal Intégration. *The interview questions were translated from French into English, and the replies translated into French by the Committee for the Republic of Canada. The interview was published on November 23, 2015, and appears here in English translation with permission.*

Intégration: Mr. Wysmuller, when did you start investigating the global climate change phenomenon, and what evidence do you have to convince our readers of the seriousness, of the rigor of your work?

Wysmuller: I've always had a love for meteorology, studied it in school, and forecasted weather at the Royal Dutch Weather Bureau in Amsterdam before working at NASA before, during, and after the Moon Landings. Mathematics that I helped develop while assigned to work at jet engine manufacturer Pratt & Whitney is being used by most climate scientists all over the world. In the late 1990s, I started lecturing on the formation of the ice ages; hence my website *The Colder Side of Global Warming.* I continue doing so to this day, and I am part of the NASA group called The Right Climate Stuff (TRCS) centered at the Johnson Space Center in Houston, Texas.

Intégration: At a recent conference in New York, you stated that after the Paris Summit on climate change, the planet will go back to the Stone Age. Can you demonstrate that to our readers?

Wysmuller: The context of that assertion was that we would revert to Stone Age conditions if every proposal, change, and energy-destroying wishlist item were to be enacted as a result of the Paris COP21 conference. It would mean that inexpensive coal-generated electricity would be barred in Africa. Developing nations would be limited to non-utility scale wind and

The Cameroonian weekly Integration *prepares its readers for the Paris "summit of depopulation."*

solar power generation. Africa, South America, and Central America would never develop continent-wide electrical grids, nor would they be permitted to develop their own natural resources. I could go on, but hopefully you are getting the idea!

Intégration: In the same vein, you are also ringing the alarm bell that behind the Paris summit lies the real agenda of some of the great powers and of some notorious people: reducing Earth's population. What are your reasons to make such a statement?

Wysmuller: Once inexpensive electrical power is denied to those most needing it, diseases will continue taking their toll in the developing world; decent drinking water will remain in short supply, and delivery systems for it will remain substandard compared to Europe and North America.

Keep in mind that there are some truly misguided but well-meaning people believing they are doing environmental good who are involved in COP21. But others want to keep the developing world poor and relying on "handouts" from the so-called "developed world."

Even our own President [Obama], a poor choice in my view, has declared that, "Ultimately, if you think about all the youth that everybody has mentioned here in Africa, if everybody is raising living standards to the point where everybody has got a car and everybody has got air conditioning, and everybody has got a big house, well, the planet will boil over—unless we find new ways of producing energy."[1]

Now this is simply false. The planet will never "boil over," unless new laws of physics get invented. But keeping Africa poor will result in more deaths from not "raising living standards."

And you should not have to wait for someone else to "find new ways of producing energy." What if they don't? Does that mean that you and your descendants should wallow in poverty?

Do *not* take our President's statement as what the American people want for your country.

For me, I would like to see every African of driving age able to

(1) have one or two cars,

(2) have a decent road system upon which to drive them,

(3) have air conditioning,

(4) have a big house or elegant apartment,

(5) have a job making, selling, or distributing things like air conditioners, cars, and farm equipment, or teaching others how to do just that, and have all those things that make life pleasant, and a lifestyle you can be proud of.

Intégration: Can you explain your statement that "global warming is not an issue that concerns Africa"?

Wysmuller: To begin: The planet's atmosphere has not warmed for almost two decades, and that includes Africa. (**Figure 1.**)

I pose the following question from time to time: Pick any day of the year, any season. Add two degrees. Notice any difference? Enjoy life. Save billions of dollars that your government wants to spend or divert on

FIGURE 1

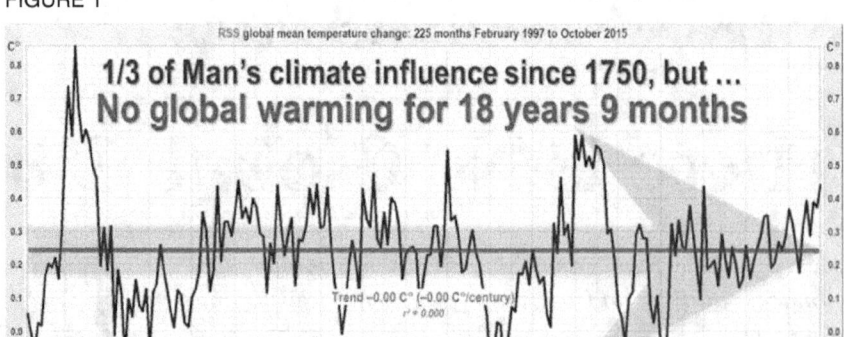

Roy Spencer, Remote Sensing Systems, Global Temperature Anomaly Troposphere/Stratosphere (TTS) data

No global warming for 18 years and 9 months. If we look at the total emissions of CO_2 produced by man since 1750, we find that one third of these emissions occurred in only the last 18 years and 9 months. However, the most reliable satellite measurements of temperature in the upper tropical troposphere—where global warming theory predicts a "hotspot" due to warming sea surface temperatures and increased tropical convection—show no indication of global warming over this period. There is no evidence to support the claims that anthropogenic CO_2 emissions are causing a sudden, dangerous change in the Earth's climate.

this foolishness.

A small fraction of those same billions could develop a power grid across all of Africa, and provide cheap, reliable, and clean coal-fired electricity for all. Increases in CO_2 would benefit the planet, allowing more rapid plant and crop growth, while carbon monoxide, carbon particles, and real pollutants would be controlled with modern engineering techniques. A competent physicist or meteorologist will tell you that Earth's equatorial regions would radiate most of that added heat into space[2]—the colder regions would warm, but not enough to cause major ice depletion. Recent evidence points to Antarctica gaining so much more ice and snow as to *drop* world sea levels by 0.23 mm each year.

Truly, global warming is not an issue that concerns Africa. Economic impoverishment most certainly is!

Intégration: Should we fear the return of colonialism, particularly in Africa?

Wysmuller: Under real colonialism, you knew from whom you wanted to be liberated. However, economic subjugation is likely even more insidious than that of your past colonial experience.

Keeping Africa from utilizing your own natural resources, keeping you without reliable power, denying you a decent transportation infrastructure to move goods throughout the continent, or even withholding reliable electrical power to make those goods, is true repression.

Don't let it happen to you!!!

Intégration: The Paris Summit organizers think that the growth of jihadism and wars in Africa is linked to global warming. What do you think?

Wysmuller: The recent unrest in the world and attacks in Paris feed this kind of thinking. In truth, poverty and lack of food and water are the fuel for jihadism. This results in destabilization attempts directed towards governments who are unable to cure these societal ills. If reliable electricity were used to power desalination plants and provide water for agriculture and industry, the attractiveness of regime destruction, relied upon by jihadists, would dissipate.

Intégration: Is there a relationship between the warming of the oceans and the emissions of CO_2?

Wysmuller: Absolutely! As the oceans warm, they release the heavier, dissolved CO_2 molecules contained within them. In fact the oceans are responsible for almost all of the CO_2 emissions added to the atmosphere every year. Humans account for less than 4%, and half of that is re-absorbed by either plants or the oceans each year!!!

Intégration: What advice would you give to the African heads of state that have already accepted the invitation to go to the Paris Summit? Should they refuse to sign the protocol to impose a worldwide climate policy?

Wysmuller: Go to the Paris Summit. Do *not* give up your nation's right to explore for, extract, utilize, and develop your natural resources.

Review any technical assistance offered, but have your own scientists who have high integrity, analyze any offers, and accept only those that

(1) give your nation capability that it doesn't presently have,

(2) contribute to your own energy independence,

(3) grant meaningful employment for your people,

(4) improve your nation's infrastructure, and

(5) allow you to increase your nation's competitiveness in all aspects of world trade.

There are many more in addition to these five, but starting with these, your heads of state will earn their right to remain in their positions.

And yes, they should absolutely refuse to sign the protocol as it has been described to me. Signing will guarantee permanent mediocrity for those African nations that are tricked into supporting the protocol.

Intégration: And what message do you have for the African population who, not long ago, heard Barack Obama tell them that it is dangerous for the planet that every house should have electricity?

Wysmuller: Tell Barack Obama to cut power to the U.S. White House 20 times per day, sell his jet plane Air Force One, and get rid of the cars that he rides in on the way to golf courses every week. When all of those happen, then consider that you might not want every house having electricity, and decide that *his* house will be the only one in that category.

Intégration: Nonetheless, the phenomenon of global warming is not a myth. And you are saying that it has some good advantages such as creating jobs?

Wysmuller: We have been in a 2-degree Centigrade (plus and minus) temperature band for the past 10,000 years! Three hundred years ago we were cooling. One hundred years ago we started warming again. We are still in that 2-degree Centigrade range, and not anywhere near the top of that range.

Add atmospheric CO_2, and plants grow more *and* need less water to do so. Satellite imagery of the Sahel region of Africa shows greening during the 20 years after the satellites were first put in orbit.

If there is any myth, it is that of taking just the past 100 years of temperature change and insisting that it will go on forever. More than 100 climate models have failed to accurately project the Earth's atmospheric temperature—and all but three failed on the high side, because of assumptions about CO_2 increase and its feedback consequences that were built into the model.

Jobs will follow as a result of *not* following the proposed resource development restrictions that some would impose upon your country while delighting in your continued subservience. I'm not one of them!!!

Intégration: The way things are going right now, some scientists fear an increase of floods, cyclones, and other natural catastrophes. Can you comment?

Wysmuller: Those scientists to whom you refer are just not keeping up with reality. I cannot apologize for their ignorance, but hopefully they can.

There is a concept called "Accumulated Cyclonic Energy" (ACE) and it is tracked worldwide. It takes the energy components of storms—wind speed, storm duration measured in 6-hour intervals, and area covered. The trend of this ACE statistic is tracked, and for the past 15 years the trend has been down, and decidedly so, even as CO_2 has risen. **(Figure 2.)**

Hurricanes, cyclones, and typhoons are within their historic ranges, though not fewer in number, but this is likely due to better satellite tracking of these systems. In areas where there is high accuracy in storm tracking, such as the United States, numbers of tornadoes in *all* categories have either diminished or are flat, none increasing!

Please keep in mind that the catastrophes referred to are all weather-related, not climate-related. Climate is the result of very long-term changes in the averages of many meteorological factors, and CO_2 is not the major one involved.

Intégration: What accounts for the fact that, two weeks before the Paris summit, the conclusions of your work and your observations are not well known around the world? Are there some people that don't want your voice to be heard?

Wysmuller: Many highly regarded and recognized scientists with world-class reputations share my outlook and have similar opinions. I give lectures, talks, and presentations all over the world, and those conclusions that I have arrived at with others are actually quite well known.

I am sure there are some that don't want my voice to be heard, but those are the actions of fear, fear that they will be exposed as less than competent, and will have to defend policies that damage the very people and nations that they claim to be helping.

Intégration: Can you tell us why you are not afraid to oppose the powerful nations and powerful people (including even the Pope) who are involved in promoting this climate change agenda? They say that that there is a danger! Are you trying to tell us that the right of all nations to develop, the need to create jobs, and the need for science to be truthful, is more important than fear?

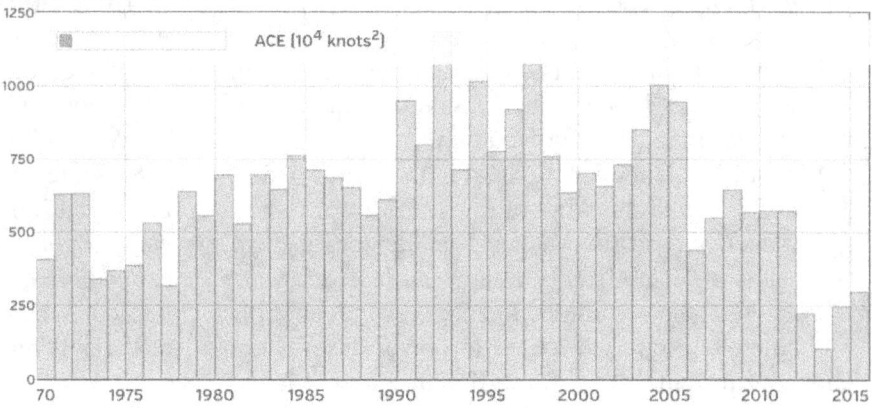

FIGURE 2

Accumulated Cyclone Energy [ACE]

Updated: November 21, 2015

ACE [10^4 knots^2]

U.S. National Oceanic and Atmospheric Administration (NOAA)

Accumulated Cyclonic Energy (ACE), a measure of the energy components of storms, has tended to decrease for the last 15 years, while CO_2 emissions have risen.

Wysmuller: Absolutely!!! And there is no "climate danger" to worry about, but there is a very real danger that lack of development, poverty, and lack of economic opportunity present to your country and the world!

I have easily developed a lack of fear with respect to my standpoint, because it is grounded in hard science, accurate data, and a structured approach to problem solving that I learned during my days at NASA. Over the years I have applied my meteorological, mathematical, and earth sciences background to my presentations and have acquired an understanding of climate and ice-age formation.

I believe my advice to the developing world will actually allow it to *develop!!!* Rise to the level that brings the best lifestyle, medical health, and prosperity that you can hope for and then benefit all of humanity!!!

When your nation's intelligence and intellect is focused on becoming equal partners in the world, the rest of the world's nations will welcome your inclusion in mainstream economic progress, and I not only look forward to that day, but will work hard to persuade others to help you achieve it.

I thank you for your work in communicating my viewpoint to your country's leaders and your general readership. Political decisions based upon sound science and correct information are the recipe for national achievement, and I wish you the very best in attaining that success!!!